(re)Defining Moments

(re)Defining Moments

---

101 KINGDOM THOUGHTS FOR LIFE-CHANGING LIVING

BOB MILLER, Ph.D., D.Min.

ServantOne
Helping Others Get To Where They Want To Go

(re)Defining Moments: 101 Kingdom Thoughts For Life-Changing Living
Copyright @ 2019 Robert D. Miller

All rights reserved. No portion of this book may be reproduced, stored in a retrieval system, or transmitted in any form or by any means—electronic, mechanical, photocopy, recording, scanning, or other—except for brief quotations in reviews or articles, without the prior written permission of the author.

Scripture taken from the New King James Version®. Copyright © 1982 by Thomas Nelson. Used by permission. All rights reserved.

Scripture taken from the New Century Version®. Copyright © 2005 by Thomas Nelson. Used by permission. All rights reserved.

Scripture quotations, unless otherwise indicated, are taken from the Holy Bible, New International Version®, NIV®. Copyright ©1973, 1978, 1984, 2011 by Biblica, Inc.™ Used by permission of Zondervan. All rights reserved worldwide. The "NIV" and "New International Version" are trademarks registered in the United States Patent and Trademark Office by Biblica, Inc.™

Scripture quotations are taken from the Holy Bible, New Living Translation, copyright ©1996, 2004, 2007, 2013 by Tyndale House Foundation. Used by permission of Tyndale House Publishers, Inc., Carol Stream, Illinois 60188. All rights reserved.

Scripture quotations are taken from THE MESSAGE. Copyright © by Eugene H. Peterson 1993, 1994, 1995, 1996, 2000, 2001, 2002. Used by permission of Tyndale House Publishers, Inc.

Scripture quotations are taken from The Living Bible copyright © 1971. Used by permission of Tyndale House Publishers, Inc., Carol Stream, Illinois 60188. All rights reserved.

Scripture quotations are from the ESV® Bible (The Holy Bible, English Standard Version®), copyright © 2001 by Crossway, a publishing ministry of Good News Publishers. Used by permission. All rights reserved.

Scripture quotations taken from the New American Standard Bible, Copyright © 1960, 1962, 1963, 1968, 1971, 1972, 1973, 1975, 1977, 1995 by The Lockman Foundation. Used by permission.

Scripture quotations taken from the Amplified Bible, Copyright © 1954, 1958, 1962, 1964, 1965, 1987 by The Lockman Foundation. Used by permission.

Scripture quotations marked HCSB are taken from the Holman Christian Standard Bible®, Copyright © 1999, 2000, 2002, 2003, 2009 by Holman Bible Publishers. Used by permission. Holman Christian Standard Bible®, Holman CSB®, and HCSB® are federally registered trademarks of Holman Bible Publishers.

Scripture taken from The Message. Copyright © 1993, 1994, 1995, 1996, 2000, 2001, 2002. Used by permission of NavPress Publishing Group. All Rights reserved. No part of this publication may be reproduced, stored in a retrieval system or transmitted in any form or by any means except for brief quotations in printed reviews, with the prior permission and consent of the author.

First Printing, 08/2019

ISBN: 9781686873195

Independently published through KDP under ServantOne

Printed in the United States of America

Readers should be aware that Internet Web sites offered as citations and/or sources for further information may have changed or disappeared between the time this was written and when it is read.

www.todaysdefiningmoment.com

ServantOne
Helping Others Get To Where They Want To Go

www.servantone.com

To Bentley, Arrington, Sammy, Aria, Anniston, Leo, Zeke, Nico, Wilder and Remington . . . and to those who may be coming a bit later: I look forward to many more defining moments as your Poppy! Your names are always written on my strong, right arm.

INTRODUCTION

I was sitting in a youth service just barely listening when George's words caught my attention. He was describing what it would be like if someone spent time alone with God every day.

I was convicted, challenged, and I'm sure some people thought it was crazy.

The next morning, I woke up early and began reading, taking notes, and asking myself the simple question, "What does God want to teach me today?"

I wish I could say that my thoughts were profound. No, they were far from it. They were proactive in establishing a pattern of purpose. Those morning times are defining moments for me. It is the time when the reality of my weaknesses meets face to face with the reason for my worship. God became part of my definition. My time with Him was deliberate, decisive, and defining.

Defining moments involve change.

Defining moments involve course correction.

Defining moments involve conviction.

Defining moments involve courage.

Greg Nemer writes, "Defining Moments bring you closer to discovering your purpose in life."[1]

Over the past years, I have written concise, practical and encouraging thoughts that have provided for my own restoration, healing and (re)defining moments.

On the following pages, you will find 101 thoughts that may bring about change, a course correction, establish a conviction, or provide you with some courage. I hope these become defining moments for you that make you passionate about your purpose in life, as they have for me. *(from Defining Moments, 2015)*

"(re)defining moment" (Noun):

An additional point at which the essential nature or character of a person is revealed or identified

KINGDOM THOUGHT 1: GRACE

But He said to me, "My grace is sufficient for you, for My power is made perfect in weakness." Therefore, I will boast all the more gladly of my weaknesses, so that the power of Christ may rest upon me. For the sake of Christ, then, I am content with weaknesses, insults, hardships, persecutions, and calamities. For when I am weak, then I am strong.
2 Corinthians 12:9-10 ESV

I've always struggled with a clear definition of "grace".

I recall the acronym from my early years, "God's Riches At Christ's Expense". It has been said that grace is the "divine influence to inspire virtuous impulses, and to impart strength to endure trial and resist temptation." In some theological circles, grace has been defined as "the love and mercy given to us by God because God desires us to have it, not because of anything we have done to earn it".

There is "common grace", "free grace", "irresistible grace", "prevenient grace", "Sola Gratia" . . . and "Amazing Grace."

The text of the most loved hymn was penned by clergyman John Newton in 1779. The melody was first published fifty years later by Charles H. Spilman and Benjamin Shaw with the title, "New Britain". The lyrics and melody were put together in 1835 by composer William Walker to form the time-tested

> "Amazing grace, how sweet the sound,
> that saved a wretch like me.
> I was once lost, but now I'm found.
> Was blind, but now I see".

Historian Jonathan Aitken estimates that this song is sung over 10 million times each year.[2]

Let's consider His grace today . . .

Grace In Salvation. A. W. Tozer writes, "The cross is the lightning rod of grace that short-circuits God's wrath to Christ so that only the light of His love remains for believers".[3] Paul reminds the Ephesians, *"For by grace you have been saved through faith. And this is not your own doing; it is the gift of God, not a result of works, so that no one may boast."* (Eph 2:8-9 ESV) God gives grace and we get God. It's His love in our lostness. He gives peace to our greatest perplexity. To Christ followers in Rome, Paul writes, *"Now that we have been put right with God through faith, we have peace with God through our Lord Jesus*

Christ. He has brought us by faith into this experience of God's grace, in which we now live. And so we boast of the hope we have of sharing God's glory!" (Rom 5:12 GNT)

Grace In Suffering. In our hurt, in our pain, in our anguish . . . God pours out the gift of His grace. Peter encourages us with these words, *"And after you have suffered a little while, the God of all grace, who has called you to his eternal glory in Christ, will Himself restore, confirm, strengthen, and establish you."* (I Peter 5:10 ESV) In his own life, Paul faced debilitating suffering. He finally surrendered to God's sufficiency, *"Three different times I begged the Lord to take it away. Each time he said, 'My grace is all you need. My power works best in weakness.' So now I am glad to boast about my weaknesses, so that the power of Christ can work through me."* (2 Cor 12:8-9 NLT) Take a moment and let that sink in . . . "My grace is all you need."

Grace In Struggles. Jesus tells us that in this world we will have trouble and struggles. (John 16:33) In our overwhelming adversity, we have unlimited access. The writer of Hebrews gives us an incredible insight, *"This High Priest of ours understands our weaknesses, for He faced all of the same testings we do, yet He did not sin. So, let us come boldly to the throne of our gracious God. There we will receive his mercy, and we will find grace to help us when we need it most."* (Heb 4:15-16 NLT) In The Message, Eugene Peterson illustrates this thought, *"Now that we know what we have - Jesus, this great High Priest with ready access to God - let's not let it slip through our fingers. We don't have a priest who is out of touch with our reality. He's been through weakness and testing, experienced it all—all but the sin. So let's walk right up to Him and get what He is so ready to give. Take the mercy, accept the help."* It's been said that running to God is grace . . . running from God is guilt.

Grace Is Sufficient. Paul reminds us, *"But He said to me, 'My grace is sufficient for you, for My power is made perfect in weakness.'"* (2 Cor 12:9). God's grace is never too little or never too much. It's exactly what we need, when we need it. God's timing is perfect. And, it's in our weaknesses that we experience God's wonder. Author Jerry Bridges encourages us, "Your worse days are never so bad that you're beyond the reach of God's grace. And, your best days are never so good that you're beyond the need of God's grace."[4]

His grace is simple, significant and sufficient.

Alexander Whyte, a Scottish Anglican writes, "Grace, then, is grace . . . that is to say, it is sovereign, it is free, it is sure, it is unconditional, and it is everlasting"[5] . . . and, it's ours!

It's God's "love and mercy given to us because God desires us to have it, not because of anything we have done to earn it". We can't earn it . . . we can only embrace it. It truly is AMAZING!

KINGDOM THOUGHT 2: FRIEND

For the Lord your God is living among you. He is a Mighty Savior. He will take delight in you with gladness. With His love, He will calm all your fears. He will rejoice over you with joyful songs.
Zephaniah 3:17 NLT

In 1995, Randy Newman wrote the lyrics for "You've Got A Friend In Me". This "Toy Story" theme song reminds us, "When the road looks rough ahead, and you're miles and miles from your nice warm bed, you just remember what your old pal said, 'Boy, you've got a friend in me.'"

Many go through life never finding that kind of friend. We long to have someone in our lives who through struggles, stupidity, sorrow and success . . . will love us and never let go.

For us, God's love is that kind of love. Jesus tells us, "I no longer call you slaves, because a master doesn't confide in his slaves. Now you are my friends, since I have told you everything the Father told me." (John 15:15 NLT)

The prophet Zephaniah tells the nation of Israel about a Mighty Savior . . . the Warrior for our soul . . . a Faithful Friend Who loves us to and through the end. He is One Who takes delight in us, Who calms our fears with His love, and Who sings over us with songs of joy.

The children's song got it right . . . His love for us is deep and wide. We experience this extraordinary love in hundreds of ways . . . here are just a few.

His Compassion. He loved us so much that "He gave His only Son". (John 3:16 NIV). "While we were yet sinners, Christ died for us." (Rom 5:8 NIV). And, when we were dead in our sin, *"God, being rich in mercy, because of the great love with which He loved us . . . made us alive together with Christ."* (Eph 2:4-5 ESV)

His Care. Even in our deepest despair, our darkest defeat or our doubtful decision, He is there with loving and longing care. Peter, the disciple who may have disappointed Jesus the most wrote, *"Humble yourselves, therefore, under the mighty hand of God so that at the proper time He may exalt you, casting all your anxieties on Him, because He cares for you."* (1 Pet 5:6-7 ESV)

His Commitment. His love is so comprehensive that nothing can change it. Paul reminds us, "For I am sure that neither death nor life, nor angels nor rulers, nor things present nor things to come, nor powers, nor height nor depth, nor anything else in all creation, will be able to separate us from the love of God in Christ Jesus our Lord." (Rom 8:38-39 ESV). No matter what challenges you face or conflicts you experience, God's love will never change.

His Companionship. Rick Warren writes, "He didn't need us. But he wanted us. And that is the most amazing thing."[6] Jesus calls us His friends, *"There is no greater love than to lay down one's life for one's friends. You are my friends if you do what I command."* (John 15:13-14 NIV). As the truest friend, He promises His never-ending presence. The author of Hebrews tells us to not be controlled by passion for anything other than God. He records the thoughts of God, "I will never fail you. I will never abandon you." (Heb 13:5 NLT) He is that *"friend"* that stays closer than a brother. (Prov 18:24)

His compassion, His care, His commitment and His companionship are yours.

Augustine writes, "God loves each of us as if there were only one of us."[7] You are the one and you will always be loved.

Our God says to each of us, "You've got a friend in me" . . . and He's a friend forever.

KINGDOM THOUGHT 3: TROPHIES

But these assets I have come to regard as liabilities because of Christ. More than that, I now regard all things as liabilities compared to the far greater value of knowing Christ Jesus my Lord, for whom I have suffered the loss of all things – indeed, I regard them as dung! – that I may gain Christ.
Philippians 3:7-8 NET

Several years ago, we sold our home and moved into a much smaller house. It's where we raised our girls for over 21 years so, we had collected a lot of stuff. The closing process provided us with plenty of opportunity to clean out closets, attics, basement and other storage areas. I was amazed at all we had acquired . . . and never got rid of.

The "purging" process was overwhelming. Finding everything, determining its value and then deciding if we wanted to keep it . . . it was paralyzing. Clothes, books, memorabilia, toys (don't even ask about the Beanie Babies), the girl's old school papers . . . I needed a recovery program for hoarders. And, because of moving into less space, we needed to get rid of some items that we liked, wanted to keep, and even enjoyed . . . but, there wasn't room in our lives for them, anymore.

We often measure effectiveness and impact by things accomplished, acquired or attained. Like that deer mount on the wall or an award on a shelf, we archive these items as examples of what we can do or evidence of we have done.

At times, these "trophies" become a badge of success, blanket of security or a banner of significance.

We wield the importance, while the apostle Paul wrestled with the impotence of these endeavors. In Philippians, Peterson captures Paul's thoughts, *"The very credentials these people are waving around as something special, I'm tearing up and throwing out with the trash—along with everything else I used to take credit for. And why? Because of Christ. Yes, all the things I once thought were so important are gone from my life."* (Phil 3:7-8 MSG)

To appreciate the power and permanence of God's Kingdom, we abandon the piety and pettiness of our own. We must make room for the right stuff.

Living with this kind of purposeful determination requires giving up, letting go and not holding on.

Hands Up - I Give Up: Surrender. I hate the implications of that word. It often is associated with defeat, failure, or weakness. In reference to God, I do not surrender because I have lost the battle . . . I surrender because Christ has already won the war. I willingly yield to a Greater Power, to a Higher Authority, to a Conquering King. There is little enduring value in "my kingdom", there is lasting eternal value in "His Kingdom". Paul writes, *"Compared to the high privilege of knowing Christ Jesus as my Master, firsthand, everything I once thought I had going for me is insignificant—dog dung. I've dumped it all in the trash so that I could embrace Christ and be embraced by him. I didn't want some petty, inferior brand of righteousness that comes from keeping a list of rules when I could get the robust kind that comes from trusting Christ—God's righteousness. I gave up all that inferior stuff so I could know Christ personally, experience his resurrection power, be a partner in his suffering, and go all the way with him to death itself. If there was any way to get in on the resurrection from the dead, I wanted to do it."* (Phil 3:9-11 MSG)

Hands Off - I Let Go: Letting go is tough. It means releasing a part of you. It's severing the cords of artificial worth for actual value. It's realizing that our trophies memorialize the past, while recognizing our hope and meaning is in the future. Young writes about God's cleaning out process, "[God's] main work is to clear out debris and clutter, making room for [His] Spirit to take full possession."[8] We need to collaborate and cooperate, confidently trusting our Creator.
We need to be willing to let go of anything that He chooses to take away. Paul reminds us, *"Forgetting the past and looking forward to what lies ahead, I press on to reach the end of the race and receive the heavenly prize for which God, through Christ Jesus, is calling us"* (Phil 3:13-14 NLT)

Hands Open - I'm Not Holding On: A longtime friend has often reminded me to "leave my hands open" so that when God puts something in, He can take it out at His pleasure. There is a tendency to tightly close our hand when God gives us something good, feeling the sense that it is now "mine". Once we place our grip on it, we no longer have an open hand for God to "remove and replace", as He sees fit. Too many times, we hang on tightly to our "blessings" and they eventually become a "burden". It becomes a transforming change to serve and not be served. Young writes, "Your sense of security must not rest in your possessions or things going your way. I am training you to depend on Me, alone, finding fulfillment in My presence. This entails being satisfied with much or with little, accepting either as My will for the moment. Instead of grasping and controlling, you are learning to release and receive."[9]

Be defined not by your things . . . but, by surrendering, severing and serving . . . it's the right stuff.

Hands up, hands off and hands open.

KINGDOM THOUGHT 4: THREE "P'S"

Rejoice in our confident hope. Be patient in trouble and keep on praying.
Romans 12:12 NLT

Every day we face the choice to conform or to change . . . to be the same or to be different.

Conforming is an indifferent satisfaction with our culture. Changing is an intentional shift. We are changed and transformed by refreshing and renewing the way we think.

The Apostle Paul presents a three-part strategy to shift our thinking. Each requires initiative and is intentional . . . and, each is life changing.

Perspective: **We Choose To Experience Happiness Because Of Hope**. The prophet Jeremiah reminds an enslaved nation, *"'For I know the plans I have for you,' says the LORD. 'They are plans for good and not for disaster, to give you a future and a hope.'"* (Jer 29:11 NLT) In grieving, there is good. In disaster, there is delight. In "hopelessness", there is always "hope". Our hope is in His presence. Our hope is in His provision. Our hope is in His promises. We have an eternity with Him, but we also have everyday with Him. He never leaves. He never abandons.

We praise in our confident hope.

Patience: We Choose To Endure Trials Because Of Transformation. There is a learning in our longing. The writer of Hebrews tells of our Savior's example, *"Even though Jesus was God's Son, he learned obedience from the things he suffered."* (Heb 5:8 NLT) Suffering provides us the opportunity to share with Jesus and to share about Jesus. Peter reminds us, *"Dear friends, don't be surprised at the fiery trials you are going through . . . be very glad—for these trials make you partners with Christ in His suffering, so that you will have the wonderful joy of seeing His glory when it is revealed to all the world."* (1 Pet 4:12-13 NLT) He turns our mess into a message. He turns our trials into a testimony. He transforms our grief into His glory.

We are patient in troubled times.

Petition: We Choose To Engage In Prayer Because Of Peace. Faithful prayer develops focused purpose. Approaching Him with prayer appropriates peace that guards what we think and how we feel. Paul tells us, *"Don't worry about anything; instead, pray about everything. Tell God what you need and thank Him for all He has done. Then you will experience God's peace, which exceeds* *anything we can understand. His peace will guard your hearts and minds as you live in Christ Jesus."* (Phil 4:6-7 NLT)

We keep on praying.

If we conform, we simply accept the way things are . . . if we change, we spiritually adapt to the way things could be. Paul says it this way, *"Don't copy the behavior and customs of this world, but let God transform you into a new person by changing the way you think. Then you will learn to know God's will for you, which is good and pleasing and perfect."* (Rom12:2 NLT)

Perspective. Patience. Prayer.

He will change your life . . . and He will make you a life changer.

Keep on praying . . .

Kingdom Thought 5: Rest

And He said, "My presence will go with you, and I will give you rest."
Exodus 33:14 ESV

I remember the first time I watched "The Ten Commandments"? Charlton Heston portrayed Moses, the emancipator of Israel. The nation of Israel suffered under Egypt's tyrannical and brutal enslavement. Under Moses' leadership they escaped by the miraculous and mighty hand of Jehovah.

God was guiding. God was giving. God was gracious.

As Moses interacted with God, the Almighty would *"speak to Moses face to face, as a man speaks to his friend."* (Ex 33:11) This process took time. When the nation grew impatient and concerned over God's intent, they allowed their hearts to fail and followed Aaron by making a golden calf to worship. Their disobedience was declared, and their future was fearful. A Holy God was not pleased.

Moses, as a wise and willing leader petitioned and pleaded with God for His powerful, protecting and prevailing presence. God answered, *"My presence will go with you, and I will give you rest."* (Ex 33:14)

Real rest is only possible in His presence. Rest is release, renewal and refreshment. The presence of God is powerful with Old Testament faith seekers and New Testament faith finders. He gives rest.

Rest From Worry. Paul reminds the Christ-followers of Philippi, *"Don't worry about anything; instead, pray about everything. Tell God what you need and thank him for all He has done."* (Phil 4:6 NLT) His ever abiding, ever attentive and ever acknowledged presence allows us the privilege of prayer. The writer of Hebrews encourages us with unlimited access to the Almighty, *"So let us come boldly to the throne of our gracious God. There we will receive His mercy, and we will find grace to help us when we need it most."* (Heb 4:16 NLT)

Rest From Weariness. Jesus speaks refreshing words to those who are weary, *"Come to Me, all of you who are weary and carry heavy burdens, and I will give you rest."* (Matt 11:28 NLT) It's easy to fall, fail and be fatigued when we walk in weariness. Our rest and replenishment are realized in His presence. Matthew continues Jesus' thought, *"Take My yoke upon you. Let Me teach you, because I am humble and gentle at heart, and you will find rest for your souls."* (Matt 11:29 NLT)

Rest From Wandering. The Israelites would find rest from years of wandering with Jehovah as their Rock. Resting in the Him gives us a reassuring residence in the Rock of our salvation. The psalmist writes, *"The LORD is my rock and my fortress and my deliverer, My God, my rock, in whom I take refuge."* (Ps 18:2 ESV). He is our solidity, safety and security. There is a distinctiveness derived from resting in Him. Moses asks God, *"For how shall it be known that I have found favor in your sight, I and Your people? Is it not in your going with us, so that we are distinct, I and Your people, from every other people on the face of the earth?"* (Ex 33:16 ESV) We are different and unique because of His devotion and undying love.

Is this a day of worry?

Is this a day of weariness?

Is this a day of wandering?

He gives rest from all of these in His presence.

Find Him . . . find rest.

KINGDOM THOUGHT 6: EYES AHEAD

Keeping our eyes fixed on Jesus, the Pioneer and Perfecter of our faith. For the joy set out for Him He endured the cross, disregarding its shame, and has taken His seat at the right hand of the throne of God.
Hebrews 12:2 NIV

I'm sure you've heard the adage, "don't blink or you'll miss it". Blinking is an auto reflex that helps our eyes stay focused. Researchers tells us that we blink 16 times a minute or almost 28,000 times in a 24-hour day.[10] That's a lot of "blinky blinky."

The writer of Hebrews reminds us that as we "run" through life (Heb 12:1), we focus on the Example as much as the ending finish line, we look for the Helper as we live for the hope, and we see Jesus in every step of the journey.

Eyes Fixed. Have you ever been in amusement park and seen groups of "first-timers" have their guide wave a identifying flag or shout out, "eyes on me"? These "newbies" can easily be distracted or detoured with never before seen sights and sounds. Cambridge implies that "fixing" is, "the concentration of the wandering gaze into a single direction."[11] In our walk, distractions take us off task and detours take us off target. Jesus tells us, "eyes on Me". We focus or "fix" our sight on our Savior. He set the example for enduring suffering from the cross and disregarding shame from critics.

Eyes Forward. Solomon gives wise instruction, *"Let your eyes look directly forward, and your gaze be straight before you."* (Prov 4:25 ESV) When Peter was given a chance to confirm his commitment to Christ's call by taking a walk on the water, he became consumed with the chaos and calamity on all sides. Matthew writes, *"And Peter answered him, 'Lord, if it is you, command me to come to you on the water.' He said, 'Come'. So Peter got out of the boat and walked on the water and came to Jesus. But when he saw the wind, he was afraid, and beginning to sink he cried out, 'Lord, save me.'"* (Matt 14:28-30 NIV) In our confusion, confidence and courage come by keeping our eyes on Christ. As Joshua led the nation of Israel, he was encouraged, *"Be strong and very courageous. Be careful to obey all the instructions Moses gave you. Do not deviate from them, turning either to the right or to the left. Then you will be successful in everything you do."* (Josh 1:7 NLT)

Eyes Following. In another translation, the writer of Hebrews pens these words, *"looking unto Jesus, the Author and Finisher of our faith . . ."* (Heb 12:2 NASB). Scripture encourages us to follow Jesus' every move, to walk by faith (2

Cor 5:7) and to follow Him (Matt 16:24). He is the Creator and Completer . . . the Pioneer and Perfecter . . . the First and the Finisher. We're reminded, *"Think of Him who endured such opposition against himself by sinners, so that you may not grow weary in your souls and give up."* (Heb 12:3 NET)

As we face all our confusions, our concerns, our chaos and our catastrophes . . . take a moment to concentrate on Christ. Blink too much with the distractions of life and you may miss Him.

Keep eyes fixed, not looking anywhere but forward and following His lead.

KINGDOM THOUGHT 7: GOOD GIVING

They are being tested by many troubles, and they are very poor. But they are also filled with abundant joy, which has overflowed in rich generosity. For I can testify that they gave not only what they could afford, but far more. And they did it of their own free will.
2 Corinthians 8:2-3 NLT

Over the years, I have learned that I'm a "fix-it" guy. Now, don't be confused . . . I'm not a handyman. Put a tool in my hand and I could do more harm than help. But, give me a challenge or a problem and I most likely will find a solution. Give me something that is organizationally or relationally broke, and I can help fix it.

The apostle Paul tells of a solution to a problem that may not be the most practical or predictable . . . but it is extremely powerful. It's a solution that hits home.

The Christ-followers in the Macedonian churches gave to believers in Jerusalem who were in extreme need. The interesting thing is that the givers we're in deep need, themselves. Giving is something we admire and appreciate . . . but, this kind of giving is amazing.

Paul tells us that these saints, who were most likely slaves and servants gave, *"in a severe test of affliction . . . and in extreme poverty."* (2 Cor 8:2 ESV)

They gave when it wasn't pleasing and when it wasn't practical. it wasn't easy and it wasn't expected.

In this poignant passage we discover several principles as to how those who really care genuinely meet needs.

Give Generously. Paul tells us that they are *"filled with abundant joy, which has overflowed in rich generosity".* (2 Cor 8:3 NLT) These gave out of their commitment and conviction, not out of their comfort. The source of their gifts was not their resources, but their reverence for God. Paul again reminds us, they gave "beyond their ability."

Give Gracefully. In his description of these servant-saints, the apostle writes, *"We want you to know, brothers, about the grace of God that has been given among the churches of Macedonia"* (2 Cor 8:1 ESV) The expression of their gift is an extension of His grace. Isn't that what true giving is all about? Giving out of grace and not out of guilt? There were no "strings attached". Even in their pain, problems and poverty . . . they understood the principle of blessings others.

Give Gratefully. Chuck Swindoll writes that this kind of giving "is much broader than money . . . it includes giving ourselves . . . our time and energy, our care and compassion, even our belongings on occasion."[12] What a unique and needed characteristic for today. Paul writes, *"They even did more than we had hoped, for their first action was to give themselves to the Lord and to us, just as God wanted them to do."* (2 Cor 8:5 NLT) We're reminded, *"You must each decide in your heart how much to give. And don't give reluctantly or in response to pressure. 'For God loves a person who gives cheerfully.'"* (2 Cor 9:7 NLT)

I appreciate Eugene Peterson's insights as written in The Message, *"Fierce troubles came down on the people of [the Macedonian churches, pushing them to the very limit. The trial exposed their true colors: They were incredibly happy, though desperately poor. The pressure triggered something totally unexpected: an outpouring of pure and generous gifts . . . they gave offerings of whatever they could—far more than they could afford —pleading for the privilege of helping out in the relief of poor Christians."* (2 Cor 8:2-4 MSG)

These who cared showed "their true colors". In sacrificing service, they gave out of their hurt, they gave to give hope and they gave to help.

It doesn't take much . . . it just takes a moment.

It doesn't have to be big . . . just a blessing.

Look for a "redefining moment" when you . . . even out of your own hurt . . . can give generously, gracefully and gratefully.

KINGDOM THOUGHT 8: SHINE THE LIGHT

All who do evil hate the light and refuse to go near it for fear their sins will be exposed. But those who do what is right come to the light so others can see that they are doing what God wants.
John 3:20-21 NLT

The beloved song, "This Little Light Of Mine" is one of the first we sing to our children. Its message is simple, yet strong . . . light-hearted, but hard-hitting, a catchy tune with a confident truth. This little light is going to shine . . . we don't hide it under a bushel, we don't let Satan blow it out and, we let it shine 'til Jesus comes. Our little light is prominent, it's powerful and it's promising. Jesus tells us that His light is an expression of the internal . . . and evidence of the eternal.

Light Guards. Jesus teaches that light exposes and makes us aware of darkness. More importantly, those who follow light, flee darkness. One of the great indicators of one's purpose is their proximity to God's light . . . His promises, His people and His plan. Dependence is light received . . . Independence is light rejected. John reminds us, *"But if we are living in the light, as God is in the light, then we have fellowship with each other, and the blood of Jesus, his Son, cleanses us from all sin."* (1 John 1:7 NLT). If we spend time with the Light of the world and walk in the light of His word, we will be drawn to the Light. Living in truth and walking in the light is real freedom.

The Light is our protection.

Light Guides. In our personal times of grief and darkness, God promises that His Word gives us guidance and direction. The psalmist writes, *"Your word is a lamp to guide my feet and a light for my path."* (Ps 119:105 NLT) When God's Word is our hope and His Spirit is at the helm, He navigates today's steps and tomorrow's journey. David calls out to God, *"Send out Your light and Your truth; let them guide me. Let them lead me to Your holy mountain, to the place where You live."* (Ps 43:3 NLT). The light of His Word always leads to the Lord we worship.

The Light is our path.

Light Glorifies. Matthew records the teaching of Jesus, *"You are the light of the world—like a city on a hilltop that cannot be hidden. No one lights a lamp and then puts it under a basket. Instead, a lamp is placed on a stand, where it gives light to everyone in the house. In the same way, let your good deeds shine out for all to see, so that everyone will praise your Heavenly Father."* (Matt 5:14-16 NLT) If we spend time with the Light of the world and walk in the light of His word, we will draw others to the Light. The spotlight is on our Savior and not self. We don't hide it . . . we hold it high.

The Light is our praise.

The apostle Paul gives the Christ-followers of Rome an illuminated instruction, *"The night is almost gone; the day of salvation will soon be here. So, remove your dark deeds like dirty clothes, and put on the shining armor of right living."* (Rom 13:12 NLT)

We can't live in both places. We must remove the darkness and replace it with the Light.

It's time to let our light shine.

KINGDOM THOUGHT 9: SELF TALK

And I am convinced that nothing can ever separate us from God's love. Neither death nor life, neither angels nor demons, neither our fears for today nor our worries about tomorrow—not even the powers of hell can separate us from God's love. No power in the sky above or in the earth below—indeed, nothing in all creation will ever be able to separate us from the love of God that is revealed in Christ Jesus our Lord.
Romans 8:38-39 NLT

There are a number of people who promote the power of self-talk. Reach Out Australia says, "Self-talk is basically your inner voice, the voice in your mind which says things that you don't necessarily say out loud. Often self-talk happens without us even realizing it and can be a subtle running commentary going on in the background of our mind. What we say in our mind can determine a lot of how we feel about who we are."[13] There can be positive, as well as negative self-talk.

Paul indicates a different approach available to Christ-followers.

Self-talk has been used to help conform the way we think and feel about ourselves. It can be used to build a positive mental framework. It's based on how we want to see ourselves.

Scripture talk is used to confirm the truth of how God thinks and feels about us. It builds a purposeful mental and spiritual framework. It's based in how God sees us.

Here's a key foundational piece of Scripture talk . . . NOTHING CAN SEPARATE US FROM GOD'S LOVE.

Here are some reminders:

Approval. God not only loves us, He likes us. He has us engraved, maybe even tattooed in the palm of His hand. He reminds us, *"See, I have inscribed you on the palms of My hands; Your walls are continually before Me."* (Is 49:16 NKJV)

Appreciation. He values us. He loves us so much that He offers His only Son's life in order to provide us with access to His eternal family. Paul writes, *"But God showed his great love for us by sending Christ to die for us while we were still sinners."* (Rom 5:8 NLT)

Acceptance. Knowing our weaknesses and faults, He still loves us. His love is founded in His grace, not our efforts. Paul gives these encouraging words, *"God saved you by His grace when you believed. And you can't take credit for this; it is* *a gift from God . . . For we are God's masterpiece. He has created us anew in Christ Jesus, so we can do the good things he planned for us long ago."* (Eph 2:8,10 NLT)

Anxiety. Through prayer and gratitude, trusting in Him, we can experience His peace that protects our feelings and our thoughts. Paul reminds us, *"Don't worry about anything; instead, pray about everything. Tell God what you need and thank Him for all He has done. Then you will experience God's peace, which exceeds anything we can understand. His peace will guard your hearts and minds as you live in Christ Jesus."* (Phil 4:6-7 NLT)

Abandonment. He will never go away. He will never give up. He will never get out. He is the Father to the fatherless. God is there for the long haul. God tells Joshua, *"No one will be able to stand against you as long as you live. For I will be with you as I was with Moses. I will not fail you or abandon you."* (Josh 1:5 NLT). The scribe of Hebrews links God's commitment to our contentment. He writes, *"Keep your lives free from the love of money and be content with what you have, because God has said, 'Never will I leave you; never will I forsake you.'"* (Heb 13:5 NIV)

Let your self-talk be Scripture talk. Take a moment and offer this prayer . . . "Jesus, I know that nothing I do, nothing I think, nothing I say or nothing I feel . . . NOTHING . . . will make You love me any less or love me anymore. You will never stop loving me."

That's power. That's purpose. That's a promise.

Kingdom Thought 10: Me Selfish?

Don't be selfish; don't try to impress others. Be humble, thinking of others as better than yourselves. Don't look out only for your own interests, but take an interest in others, too.
Philippians 2:3-4 NLT

Selfishness is one of those "soft" sins that has significant impact.

We all struggle with the sentiments, "I just want to be happy", "I deserve something better " or "I have earned this". Selfishness shifts the focus from God's purpose to our own pleasure, possessions or position. It's easy replacing surrender with self.

Selfishness is characteristic of our soul's enemy . . . to kill, steal and destroy. Our Savior's emphasis is to live a life of abundant satisfaction. (John 10:10)

Selfishness is life-grabbing. Selflessness is life-giving. Fromm states, "Selfish persons are incapable of loving others, but they are not capable of loving themselves either."[14]

Selfishness Demonstrates Fear. Focusing on self builds walls, as opposed to bridges. Giving is rooted in faith . . . getting is a result of fear. God's perfected affection counteracts our personal acquisitiveness. Matthew Henry comments, "If you expect or experience the benefit of God's compassions to yourselves, be compassionate one to another."[15] John writes, *"There is no fear in love. But perfect love drives out fear, because fear has to do with punishment. The one who fears is not made perfect in love."* (1 John 4:18 NIV). Compassion defeats our covetousness.

Selfishness Delivers Failure. A lack of love always leads to loss. The prophet Jeremiah writes, *"Should you then seek great things for yourself? Do not seek them . . ."* (Jer 45:5 NIV). When we only consider our own interest, we become indifferent to others. When selfishness runs without restraint families are fractured, businesses are bankrupt, and relationships are ruined. Richard Whately writes, "A man is called selfish not for pursuing his own good, but for neglecting his neighbor's."[16] Paul reminds us, *"But for those who are self-seeking and who reject the truth and follow evil, there will be wrath and anger."* (Rom 2:8 NIV).

Selfishness Defines Fraud. James challenges us, *"For where you have envy and selfish ambition, there you find disorder and every evil practice."* (Jam 3:16 NIV). Pope John Paul II writes, "The great danger for family life, in the midst of any society whose idols are pleasure, comfort and independence, lies in the fact that people close their hearts and become selfish."[17] A disingenuous life always leads to deceit.

T. W. Manson reminds us, "In the Kingdom of God, service is not a stepping-stone to nobility: it is nobility, the only kind of nobility that is recognized."[18] Paul tells us, *"For you were called to freedom, brothers and sisters; only do not use your freedom as an opportunity to indulge your flesh, but through love serve one another."* (Gal 5:13 NET)

The only cure for selfishness is surrendering to the selfless Savior and serving others. His example encourages us to live in humility, think of others more than we think of ourselves, and to take an interest them.

Kingdom Thought 11: Show Me The Love

This is real love—not that we loved God, but that He loved us and sent His Son as a sacrifice to take away our sins. Dear friends, since God loved us that much, we surely ought to love each other.
1 John 4:10-11 NLT

John Bolloten is a reggae musician and DJ based in Bradford, England known as "The Rootsman".

Bolloten writes the following lyrics for his song, "Show Me Some Love":

> *"Show some love to each and every one.*
> *Feed the children and do no wrong.*
> *Help the weak and the strong.*
> *Love your neighbor as yourself.*
> *And everything will be right in His sight.*
> *Love, show some love."*

The love of God is a life-changing, live-giving and life-impacting experience.

Love moves us from getting to giving.

Paul writes to believers in Ephesus, *"Once you were dead because of your disobedience and your many sins . . . But God is so rich in mercy, and He loved us so much, that even though we were dead because of our sins, He gave us life when He raised Christ from the dead. It is only by God's grace that you have been saved!"* (Eph 2:1, 4-5 NLT). Receiving God's love requires responding with God's love.

The followers in Corinth needed to redefine a response of love. These believers embraced persuasive speaking, powerful faith, personal sacrifice or philanthropy as evidences of love, yet Paul tells that these are all ineffective and impotent without an expression of love. (1 Cor 13:1-3)

Old habits . . . like old responses . . . are hard to break. Paul gives some very practical insight into leaving old customs and living in new compassion.

Impatience Disappoints. The apostle writes, *"Love is patient and kind."* (1 Cor 13:4 ESV). This is a tough one. We live in an immediate response world. Fast food is never quick enough. Someone is always driving slow in the fast lane. And, no one ever has "15 items or less" in the grocery store's express aisle. Losing patience never delivers the results we want . . . it only disappoints. Paul describes our walk and worthy calling this way, *"Always be humble and gentle. Be patient with each other, making allowance for each other's faults because of your love."* (Eph 4:2 NLT)

Authentic love takes time to give time.

Jealously Destroys. Paul continues, *"Love is not jealous"* (1 Cor 13:4 ESV) My pastor comments, "Jealously doesn't hurt others, it hurts us."[19] Often our intent is to build ourselves up while we tear others down. Demolition is always destructive. James writes, *"But if you are bitterly jealous and there is selfish ambition in your heart, don't cover up the truth with boasting and lying. For jealousy and selfishness are not God's kind of wisdom. Such things are earthly, unspiritual, and demonic"*. (James 3:14-15 NLT).

Authentic love appreciates the accomplishments of others.

Rudeness Disrespects. The Holman Commentary gives some insight into this passage, "At the heart of rudeness is a disregard for the social customs that others have adopted. When one does not concern himself with the likes and dislikes of others, he shows a disrespect for them." Paul highlights this thought, *"Love is not . . . boastful or proud or rude."* (1 Cor 13:4-5 NLT) Rudeness is a result of pride. We end up thinking more of ourselves than we should. Solomon warns us, *"Pride goes before destruction, and a haughty spirit before a fall."* (Proverbs 16:18 NET) Paul reminds the believers in Rome, "Because of the privilege and authority God has given me, I give each of you this warning: Don't think you are better than you really are. Be honest in your evaluation of yourselves, measuring yourselves by the faith God has given us." (Rom 12:3 NLT)

Authentic love thinks of others first.

Patience to all. Happy for others. Kind and humble. That's what love is . . . and that's what it looks like.

Let's show some love, today.

KINGDOM MOMENT 12: NOT QUALIFIED

But Moses pleaded with the Lord, "O Lord, I'm not very good with words. I never have been, and I'm not now, even though You have spoken to me. I get tongue-tied, and my words get tangled." . . . Now go! I will be with you as you speak, and I will instruct you in what to say.
Exodus 4:10, 12 NLT

How many times have we been in Moses' situation . . . God says "go" and we say "no"?

It's not because we are disobedient . . . it's because we are discouraged.

It's not because we don't think God can do it . . . it's because we think God can't do it through us.

We don't question His authority; we question our ability.

Moses was promised confidence and content . . . God would be with him and teach him what to say. Yet, Moses still doubted his divine appointment.

Reverend Micheal Beckwith says, "God doesn't call the qualified, He qualifies the called."[20] It's not uncommon for God to use common cracked pots to do Kingdom work. Those who are the most skilled are usually the least selected.

Jacob was a cheater.
Peter had a temper.
David had an affair.
Noah got drunk.
Jonah ran from God.
Paul was responsible for the murder of Christians.
Gideon was insecure.
Miriam was a gossip.
Martha was a worrier.
Thomas was a doubter.
Sarah was impatient.
Elijah was moody.
Moses stuttered.
Abraham was old.
Job went bankrupt.
The woman at the well was divorced.
Peter lied about knowing Jesus.
And, Lazarus . . . well, he was dead.

God doesn't call the qualified, He qualifies the called!

He Confirms Our Call. Paul writes, *"Therefore I, a prisoner for serving the Lord, beg you to lead a life worthy of your calling, for you have been called by God. Always be humble and gentle. Be patient with each other, making allowance for each other's faults because of your love. Make every effort to keep yourselves united in the Spirit, binding yourselves together with peace"* (Eph 4:1-3 NLT) Our call is confirmed when we answer with humble hearts, grateful gentleness and practicing peace. Loving others with our service and unity within the Body of Christ are the evidences of our everyday and eternal efforts.

He Affirms Our Adequacy. God loves taking a rag-tag team and giving them a righteous triumph. Paul reminds the Christ followers in Corinth of God's recruiting strategy, *"But God chose what the world thinks foolish to shame the wise, and God chose what the world thinks weak to shame the strong. God chose what is low and despised in the world, what is regarded as nothing, to set aside what is regarded as something, so that no one can boast in his presence."* (1 Cor 1:27-29 NET). We may not bring much to the table, but what we do bring, God blesses and uses.

He Works Through Our Weakness. God's grace works in our greatest weakness. The apostle Paul experienced this gift of grace, *"Each time He said, 'My grace is all you need. My power works best in weakness.' So now I am glad to boast about my weaknesses, so that the power of Christ can work through me. That's why I take pleasure in my weakness . . . For when I am weak, then I am strong."* (2 Cor 12:9-10 NLT) Paul reminds the faithful in Philippi, *"For I can do everything through Christ, who gives me strength."* (Phil 4:13 NLT). Our weakness does not allow us to give up, but to give in . . . to God's promised power and purpose.

Life can be discouraging, disillusioning and disappointing . . . but, don't give up on God's calling. He has sovereignly selected you for service. He will confirm you. He will affirm you. And, He will work through you.

He qualifies the convicted, the compassionate, the contrite and the called. He will qualify you.

Kingdom Thought 13: Contentment

But godliness with contentment is great gain.
1 Timothy 6:6 NIV

Sometimes we're just all over the "happiness" map. Satisfaction and fulfillment seem to come from many different sources, yet none are truly satisfying or fulfilling. Our need for more satisfaction can lead to meaningless searching.

Contentment is defined as "happiness with one's situation in life." Yet, our contentment is often conditional on our circumstances, our checking account or our comfort.

Author Rob Kuban writes, "The Bible calls us to allow our convictions, not our circumstances, to govern our sense of contentment. True, biblical contentment is a conviction that Christ's power, purpose and provision is sufficient for every circumstance. We are to learn how to walk through all kinds of adversity believing in and experiencing Christ's sufficiency. We have to choose to rest on God's good promises despite what may be going on in our lives."[21] What a thought . . . we choose to rest in God's promise.

Contentment Is Rejoicing. The Chinese philosopher Laozi writes, "Be content with what you have; rejoice in the way things are. When you realize there is nothing lacking, the whole world belongs to you."[22] Paul reminds the Christ-followers in Philippi, *"Always be full of joy in the Lord. I say it again—rejoice!"* (Phil 4:4 NLT) He continues to give his reason for rejoicing, *"Not that I am speaking of being in need, for I have learned in whatever situation I am to be content."* (Phil 4:11 ESV). Simply, we decide to delight.

Contentment Is Resisting. Pearl S. Buck says, "Many people lose the small joys in the hope for the big happiness."[23] Since the Garden of Eden, the enemy has tried to convince us that what we already have is not good enough . . . we need more. The writer of Hebrews reminds us that Jesus is enough, *"Keep your life free from love of money, and be content with what you have, for He has said, 'I will never leave you nor forsake you.'"* (Heb 13:5 ESV)

Contentment Is Resolve. A conviction to be content directs our decisions. Paul writes of his own resolution and conviction to the believers in Corinth, *"For the sake of Christ, then, I am content with weaknesses, insults, hardships, persecutions, and calamities. For when I am weak, then I am strong."* (2 Cor. 12:10 ESV). In his difficulties, Paul decides to be content.

Here is someone's "commitment of contentment" that was recently posted, "I do solemnly resolve to embrace my current season of life and will maximize my time in it. I will resist the urge to hurry through or circumvent any portion of my journey but will live with a spirit of contentment."

This is our defining prayer of conviction and commitment . . . say it with me, "I will Rejoice. I will Resist. And, I will be Resolved . . . I am content."

KINGDOM THOUGHT 14: HE'S SINGING

For the Lord your God is living among you. He is a mighty Savior. He will take delight in you with gladness. With His love, He will calm all your fears. He will rejoice over you with joyful songs.
Zephaniah 3:17 NLT

The prophet Zephaniah's words illustrate the nation of Israel's future promise and identify our present potential. We often need to be reminded that God is not just residing in us . . . He is "doing life" with us and through us. In our desperation and discouragement, we need to be reminded of our Deliverer.

He conquers our conflict.

He delights in our devotion.

He brings gladness to our grief.

He is calm in our confusion.

His presence is not passive, but purposeful and provides a peace. As God living among us becomes more evident, the benefit is more experienced.

He Saves. The psalmist writes, *"Who is this King of glory? The LORD, strong and mighty, the LORD, mighty in battle!"* (Ps 24:8 NLT). As He defeated the enemy of our soul, He delivered us in salvation. The writer to the Hebrews reminds us, *"Therefore He [Jesus] is able to save completely those who come to God through Him, because He always lives to intercede for them."* (Heb 7:25 NIV) Hillsong gives us this truth in a powerful song,

"My Savior, He can move the mountains,

My God is Mighty to save, He is Mighty to save.

Forever, Author of salvation,

He rose and conquered the grave, Jesus conquered the grave."

He Soothes. The prophet confirms God's compassion. He says, *"With His love, He will calm all your fears."* Exell and Spence-Jones write, "This is a human expression, denoting that perfect love which needs no outward demonstration. For the very greatness of His love God rests, as it were, in quiet enjoyment of it."[24] The depth of God's love deafens any distractions. His passion gives us peace. Paul reminds the Christ-followers in Rome, *"And I am convinced that nothing can ever separate us from God's love. Neither death nor life, neither angels nor demons, neither our fears for today nor our worries about tomorrow—not even the powers of hell can separate us from God's love."* (Rom 8:38 NLT) His love is unshakable, unstoppable and unseperatable.

He Sings. One of the great pleasures of parenting is holding a child while singing songs of promise, songs of peace and songs of passion. The prophet reminds us that the "God who lives among you" will "rejoice over you with joyful songs". Imagine what it would be like to hear the voice of God singing "I am your hiding place" . . . "You are an overcomer" . . . "You will never be alone" . . . "You once were lost, but now you're found". No assumption . . . only assurance. His repertoire is endless. The psalmist writes, *"You are a hiding place for me; You preserve me from trouble; You surround me with songs of deliverance."* (Psalm 32:7 NASB). Our God is composing songs for our comfort, for our conflicts and for our confidence . . . can you hear Him?

Jehovah God is strong enough to save and sensitive enough to serenade.

He lives with you. He loves you. And, listen . . . He's singing to you.

KINGDOM THOUGHT 15: SHE'S EXCELLENT

An excellent wife who can find. She is far more precious than jewels.
Proverbs 31:10 ESV

The first known use of this word was in the 14th Century . . . *Excellent* . . . "Of the highest quality, surpassing the norm, a achieving a standard of superior characteristics."

To conclude his most exhaustive published work on wisdom, Solomon writes about the qualities and characteristics of an "excellent wife". He uses ink and scroll to describe the ideal spouse. From experience, Solomon had some pretty extensive research from which to draw his conclusions . . . 300 wives and 700 paramours? Oh my!!!

She's Strong. A woman deceived and defeated one of the strongest men in the biblical history. The Almighty, all-powerful Son of God was delivered into this world by a young virgin. One of Israel's great kings was weakened by a woman bathing on a rooftop. Positive and problematic, stories of powerful women are seen throughout scripture. Yet, Solomon differentiates between power and strength. He writes, *"She is clothed with strength and dignity, and she laughs without fear of the future."* (Prov 31:25 NLT). Her strength is highlighted by dignity . . . her power has purpose and promise.

She Serves. Solomon describes an "excellent wife" as one with a heart of healing and hope, *"She extends a helping hand to the poor and opens her arms to the needy."* (Prov 31:20 NLT). This woman is ready to share her time, talent and treasure to meet the needs of those who trust in her. Solomon gives some insight, *"She gets up before dawn to prepare breakfast for her household and plan the day's work for her servant girls."* (Prov 31:15 NLT)

She Supplicates. Hannah prayed for Samuel. (1 Sam 1:10). Mary prayed as a young, expectant mother of a coming Savior and *"treasured these things in her heart"* (Luke 2:9). Our daughters prayed for the children they have carried. A mom's intercession is intentional and intimate. Abraham Lincoln writes, "I remember my mother's prayers and they have always followed me. They have clung to me all my life."[25] A praying mother is a power that is never passive.

She Speaks. Her words are timely, true and encouraging. Solomon writes, *"When she speaks, her words are wise, and she gives instructions with kindness."* (Proverbs 31:26 NLT)

She Satisfies. Although there are challenges, conflicts and chaos, there is a confident comfort. This wise man reminds us, "Her children stand and bless her. Her husband praises her: 'There are many virtuous and capable women in the world, but you surpass them all!'" (Prov 31:29 NLT)

This is a pretty high standard. Many consider Solomon's words and may be overwhelmed. Like our walk of faith . . . this becomes a goal only attainable by grace. God works on us as we walk with Him.

Three thoughts . . .

Aspire. As a father of four daughters, I appreciate their aspiration to excellence. Young women and young moms need to find an "excellent" coach, mentor and journey-walker. Find the women you admire and follow.

Affirm. To all who have wonderful women in their lives, affirmation is a powerful reminder of love and honor. Acknowledging areas of excellence inspires.

Appreciate. We need to take time to express our thanks. I appreciate the giftedness, grace, generosity and not giving up that my wife demonstrates every day.

Solomon summed it up with these words, "*Charm is deceptive, and beauty does not last; but a woman who fears the Lord will be greatly praised. Reward her for all she has done. Let her deeds publicly declare her praise.*" (Proverbs 31:30-31 NLT)

KINGDOM THOUGHT 16: POURING GRACE

So we praise God for the glorious grace He has poured out on us who belong to his dear Son. He is so rich in kindness and grace that He purchased our freedom with the blood of His Son and forgave our sins. He has showered His kindness on us, along with all wisdom and understanding.
Ephesians 1:6-8 NLT

Have you ever had days when the freedom we have in Christ seems to be fleeting?

Are the liberties of life lost in the looming weight of worry?

Are problems only bringing pain?

Is discouragement only bringing doubt?

We are often imprisoned . . . shackled . . . suffering difficulty, hardship and discomfort.

Paul finds rest and reassurance in God's grace during his own grief. He experiences God's kindness and grace . . . grace "poured out" as a promise. As the apostle Paul sits in chains, he writes to the devoted followers of Christ who live in Ephesus encouraging them in the richness of God.

Secure In Freedom. Jesus reminds us, *"And you will know the truth, and the truth will set you free."* (John 8:32 NLT). In writing to the faithful in Rome, Paul says, *"Sin is no longer your master, for you no longer live under the requirements of the law. Instead, you live under the freedom of God's grace."* (Rom 6:14 NLT). The stronghold of the serpent has been severed by our Savior. Chains are broken by the blood of Jesus. Paul reminds us, *"So now there is no condemnation for those who belong to Christ Jesus."* (Rom 8:1 NLT)

We are free.

Sins Are Forgiven. We are not only free from the power; we are forgiven from the penalty of sin. There's an old hymn that reads, "Thank God, I am free, free, free from this world is sin." Our sin . . . our shortcomings . . . our internal struggles . . . are scoured away. Yesterday's, today's and tomorrow's wickedness are wiped clean. This is God's amazing grace. Paul writes, *"God saved you by his grace when you believed. And you can't take credit for this; it is a gift from God."* (Eph 2:8 NLT).

We are forgiven.

Showered With Kindness. The psalmist writes of God's promised faithfulness to us, *"Nevertheless My lovingkindness I will not utterly take from you, Nor allow My faithfulness to fail."* (Ps 89:33 NKJV). He is always kind. He is always tender. He is always gracious. The Apostle Paul reminds us of God's continual compassion, *"in order that in the coming ages He might show the incomparable riches of His grace, expressed in His kindness to us in Christ Jesus."* (Eph 2:7 NIV) Paul uses the word, "showered" which illustrates a drenching, abundant and satisfying rain. In the dryness of the day, God sends a shower of kindness.

We are favored.

God makes us free and forgiven through the abundance of His kindness and grace. He turns burden into blessing. Here are some encouraging lyrics from James McFall:

> *"For a long time, I travelled down a long lonely road;*
> *My heart was so heavy in sin I sank low.*
> *Then I heard about Jesus, what a wonderful hour;*
> *I'm so glad that I found out, He could bring me out*
> *Through His saving power."*

> *"Like a bird out of prison that has taken its flight;*
> *Like a blind man that God gave back his sight.*
> *Like a poor wretched beggar that's found fortune and fame,*
> *I'm so glad that I found out He could bring me out*
> *Thro' His holy name."*

> *"Thank God I am free, free, free from this world of sin.*
> *I've been washed in the blood of Jesus; I've been born again.*
> *Hallelujah, I'm saved, saved, saved by His wonderful grace.*
> *I'm so glad that I found out He could bring me out*
> *And show me the way."*[26]

Today, you are free. Today, you are forgiven. Today, you are favored.

Aren't you glad that you found out, He would bring you out and show you the way?

Kingdom Thought 17: Get Back Up

The godly may trip seven times, but they will get up again. But one disaster is enough to overthrow the wicked.
Proverbs 24:16 NLT

I loved watching Chevy Chase "tripping and falling" during his comedic routines. It was the surprise, timing and pseudo-clumsiness that made it funny. Candidly, we all have experienced an untimely and embarrassing fall that has caused a chuckle or two.

Falling down gives us an opportunity to get back up.

Solomon tells us, *"for though the righteous fall seven times, they rise again . . ."* (Prov 24:16 NIV) We are often knocked down . . . but, not knocked out. The author of proverbial wisdom identifies "getting back up" as a righteous trait. It's a reflection of the resurrection. Jesus was felled by death, yet He did not surrender . . . He did not stay defeated . . . He arose and appropriated the power of the resurrection to those who have surrendered to Him. Paul made his desire clear, *"I want to know Christ—yes, to know the power of his resurrection and participation in his sufferings . . ."* (Phil 3:10 NIV)

Perseverance. Winston Churchill said, "Success is going from one failure to the next without loss of enthusiasm."[27] There is a revealing sense of righteousness hidden within resilience. As Joshua begins to lead the nation of Israel out of wilderness and into promise, God encourages him to persevere, *"This is my command—be strong and courageous! Do not be afraid or discouraged. For the LORD your God is with you wherever you go."* (Josh 1:9 NLT). At the end of their conquest, Joshua states *"Not a single one of all the good promises the LORD had given to the family of Israel was left unfulfilled; everything he had spoken came true."* (Josh 21:45 NLT)

God's presence encourages us to persevere.

Perspective. Let's just state the obvious . . . everyone falls at some point? Paul reminds the Christ-followers in Corinth, *"If you think you are standing strong, be careful not to fall. The temptations in your life are no different from what others experience. And God is faithful. He will not allow the temptation to be more than you can stand. When you are tempted, he will show you a way out so that you can endure."* (1 Cor 10:12-13 NLT) Many find it necessary to remind others when they fall and yet forget their own missteps. Words of criticism can weigh us down. Those who taunt us cannot triumph over us. The prophet Micah writes, *"Do not gloat over me, my enemies! For though I fall, I will rise again. Though I sit in darkness, the LORD will be my light."* (Micah 7:8 NLT) Look around

. . . get a true perspective. We're not alone or abandoned.

God is faithful.

Promise. John records the words of Jesus as He explains the intent of the enemy, *"The thief's purpose is to steal and kill and destroy. My [promised purpose] is to give them a rich and satisfying life."* (John 10:10 NLT) It may seem like everything is falling apart . . . but, God . . . your God is faithful. The psalmist reminds us, *"My health may fail, and my spirit may grow weak, but God remains the strength of my heart; He is mine forever."* (Ps 73:26 NLT).

He will be with us; He will guide us and He will never leave us.

I recently viewed a video that followed the training of young winter athletes. In their early years of training, they repeatedly fell . . . and they fell a lot . . . but they always got back up. At the end of the video, the athletes delivered near perfect performances in world-class competition. The tagline at the end of the video read, "Falling down is a struggle. Getting up makes us stronger."

If you're struggling, it's time to get stronger. Don't stay down . . . you're not defeated . . . you're not done . . . you're finding today's determination. It's time to get back up . . . you have the ability and you are not alone.

It will take perseverance.

You will need to change your perspective.

And, the Lord, your God will be with you . . . He promises.

KINGDOM THOUGHT 18: IT'S A LIE

My son, give me your heart, and let your eyes observe my ways.
Proverbs 23:26 NIV

As Solomon shares insightful words of wisdom, he surmises that surrendering the heart secures the soul.

Surrender is not a willing reaction; it is a willful response.

Surrender is giving God our heart . . . our hurts . . . our hopes.

Surrender is unconditional.

Surrender is acknowledging that it's all about Jesus Christ and accepting that it's not about me.

True surrender is total submission.

I don't like to surrender.

Jesus reminds us, *"If anyone would come after Me, let him deny himself and take up his cross daily and follow Me."* (Luke 9:23 ESV)

Brent Byerman writes, "The spiritual battle takes place in our minds, but the place we give Christ in our hearts determines our victory."[28] Paul emphasizes to the faithful in Corinth, *"We demolish arguments and every pretension that sets itself up against the knowledge of God, and we take captive every thought to make it obedient to Christ."* (2 Cor 10:5 NIV)

In one of his letters, John instructs the followers of Jesus to keep themselves from idols. Another translation says, *"Dear children, keep away from anything that might take God's place in your hearts."* (1 John 5:21 NLT)

My friend, Tierce Green presents a strategy of surrender . . . a "battle-plan" that will help us "keep away from anything that might take God's place". Here are some modified thoughts of Tierce's strategy.

Admit Our Struggles. All of us struggle with an idol . . . an insecurity, ideal or influence that isolates our heart from God. Paul reminds the disciples in Galatia, *"The sinful nature wants to do evil, which is just the opposite of what the Spirit wants. And the Spirit gives us desires that are the opposite of what the sinful nature desires. These two forces are constantly fighting each other, so you are not free to carry out your good intentions."* (Gal 5:17 NLT) Talking with trustworthy friends can bring healing. James tells us, *"Confess your sins to each other and pray for each other so that you may be healed."* (James 5:16 NLT)

Acknowledge The Lies. Moses describes the destructive damage of self-deceit. He says, *"But be careful. Don't let your heart be deceived so that you turn* *away from the Lord and serve and worship other gods."* (Deut 11:16 NLT). Jesus clarifies the character of our enemy as the *"father of lies"* (John 8:44) and his commitment to *"kill, steal and destroy"*. (John 10:10) The tempter's lies tell us that we are condemned, that we are to weak or that God is not pleased with us. These lies are like a stubborn weed that must be removed by the root. My dear friend, Rusty Goodwin writes, "Satan does not follow any 'rules of engagement'".[29] Our enemy does not let up when we have had too much. He is not concerned when we are tired. He doesn't give up when we are knocked down . . . his mission is to kill . . . to steal . . . to destroy.

Apply God's Truth. Paul tells us that the only deterrent to conforming is transforming. He writes, *"Don't copy the behavior and customs of this world, but let God transform you into a new person by changing the way you think. Then you will learn to know God's will for you, which is good and pleasing and perfect."* (Romans 12:2 NLT) Jesus tells us, "If you hold to my teaching, you are really my disciples. Then you will know the truth, and the truth will set you free." (John 8:31-32 NIV)

In the early 1900's, Judson W. Van de Venter wrote the following lyrics of a most beloved hymn:

> *"All to Jesus, I surrender,*
> *All to Him, I freely give.*
> *I will ever love and trust Him,*
> *In His presence daily live."*

> *"I surrender all, I surrender all.*
> *All to Thee, my blessed Savior, I surrender all."*[30]

Admit your struggle . . . Acknowledge the lies of the enemy . . . Apply God's truth.

Give it to Him . . . SURRENDER!

Kingdom Thought 19: Good Fruit

Our people must also learn to engage in good deeds to meet pressing needs, so that they will not be unfruitful.
Titus 3:14 NLT

An aged Paul writes to a young Greek leader in the church of Crete, named Titus. Crete, an island just south of Greece in the Mediterranean Sea, was notorious for philandering, quarreling and laziness.

Paul knew the power of good works demonstrated by devoted followers of Christ . . . shifting from harmful injustice to profitable influence. He writes to Titus, *"The saying is trustworthy, and I want you to insist on these things, so that those who have believed in God may be careful to devote themselves to good works. These things are excellent and profitable for people."* (Titus 3:8 ESV) Paul gives Titus a mandate and mission.

Imperative. Paul uses the word, "must". This opportunity is not an option, but an obligation. Dr. Martin Luther King, Jr. said, "Somewhere along the way, we must learn that there is nothing greater than to do something for others."[31] When our priority is serving, our practice is sacrificial . . . when our practice is sacrificial, our potential is significant. Peterson reminds us of Paul's caution to Roman believers, *"Don't burn out; keep yourselves fueled and aflame. Be alert servants of the Master, cheerfully expectant. Don't quit in hard times; pray all the harder. Help needy Christians; be inventive in hospitality."* (Rom 12:11-13 MSG)

Instruction. Learning to "engage in good works" is something that doesn't come naturally. McGee writes, "We must 'learn' to maintain good works. It's something that must be worked at. A great many people think it is easy; we need to know what God considers good works, and we need to learn how to do them."[32] Paul instructs the believers in Rome, *"Share with the Lord's people who are in need. Practice hospitality."* (Rom 12:13 NIV). We develop the skill of serving and grow in grace by giving.

Initiative. We are to "engage" to "meet pressing needs". Luther calls these, the "urgent necessities" and "the indispensable wants". In Classic Greek literature, they are called the "necessaries of life." Paul encourages Titus to "make the first move" in meeting the most immediate and fundamental needs. We are not to wait . . . but to initiate. Paul reminds the elders from Ephesus, *"And I have been a constant example of how you can help those in need by working hard. You should remember the words of the Lord Jesus: 'It is more blessed to give than to receive.'"* (Acts 20:35 NLT). Our engagement to give provides us the experience of grace.

Intentional. It's insightful that Paul used a "double negative" by writing "so that they will not be unfruitful". In Greek syntax, the use of a double negative communicates purposeful intention. It is the "driving force" of a thought or idea. Kingdom living is intent on being fruitful. To the Christ-followers in Galatia, he writes, *"But the Holy Spirit produces this kind of fruit in our lives: love, joy, peace, patience, kindness, goodness, faithfulness, gentleness, and self-control. There is no law against these things! Those who belong to Christ Jesus have nailed the passions and desires of their sinful nature to his cross and crucified them there."* (Gal 5:22-24 NLT) Responding because of the Spirit and by the Spirit unleashes His passion and desire. Producing God's fruit becomes our purpose.

Newsong sings the following lyrics,

> *"Give yourself away, be the hands and feet of Jesus*
> *Give yourself away, go out and make a world of difference*
> *Let this be the day you see how far that His love reaches*
> *The greatest sacrifice of all is to give yourself away"*

Give yourself away . . . Good deeds . . . Giving glory to God.

That's some good fruit.

KINGDOM THOUGHT 20: ALL I NEED

Such confidence we have through Christ toward God. Not that we are adequate in ourselves to consider anything as coming from ourselves, but our adequacy is from God.
2 Corinthians 3:4-5 NASB

From our earliest recollections, we work to prove ourselves and to feel like we belong. Belonging, connecting and intimacy are some of our basic needs. In *Devotions Upon Emergent Occasions*, John Donne writes in Meditation XVII, the phrase "no man is an island". This phrase is an expression that we all are connected to others, to our surroundings and to God.

Paul expresses this same sentiment in his letter to the Christ-followers in Philippi, *"That I may know Him . . .".* (Phil 3:10 NASB). In knowing Christ, He becomes our identity and our intimacy.

We no longer "measure up" based on who we know . . . but, based in Who knows us.

What we have accomplished gives way to what has been accomplished in us through Christ.

Our qualifications are His qualifications.

Our competences are His competences.

The breadth of our identity and the depth of our intimacy is found in Christ, alone.

As Paul writes to the troubled church in Corinth, he reminds them that confidence was not found in his own ability, accomplishments or authority . . . but in God through Christ's work in him.

Be encouraged that Christ is all you need.

He Is Our Adequacy. There's a worship chorus, "Christ is all I need. Christ is all I need. All that I need." Paul understands this declaration when he writes, *"but our adequacy is from God."* To the Philippian believers he writes, *"I can do all things through Christ who gives me strength."* (Phil 4:13 NIV). As Joseph stands before Pharaoh with an impossible task of uncovering and interpreting a dream, he responds, *"'It is beyond my power to do this,' Joseph replied. 'But God can tell you what it means and set you at ease.'"* (Gen 41:16 NLT). The incompetent becomes competent through the power of God.

He Is Our Anointing. In the Old Testament, kings are recognized by an anointing of olive oil to signify their appointment and approval as God's choice to lead and confirmation of His glory. Jesus is called "The Christ" which means "The Anointed One". Paul writes to the faithful in Colossae, *"To them God chose to make known how great among the Gentiles are the riches of the glory of this mystery, which is Christ in you, the hope of glory."* (Col 1:27 ESV). The disciple John writes of our connection because of this anointing, *"But the anointing that you received from Him abides in you, and you have no need that anyone should teach you. But as His anointing teaches you about everything, and is true, and is no lie—just as it has taught you, abide in Him."* (1 John 2:27 ESV).

He Is Our Acceptance. The writer of Hebrews tells us that we have been accepted with access in our times of need, *"Let us therefore come boldly unto the throne of grace, that we may obtain mercy, and find grace to help in time of need."* (Heb 4:16 NKJV) Paul reminds the Ephesians, *"To the praise of the glory of his grace, wherein He hath made us accepted in the Beloved."* (Eph 1:6) NKJV. We are accepted because Jesus paid the price for our admission to THE Family.

Today, rest in the realization that you don't need to do anything more . . . it's already been done.

Because of Christ we belong, we are blessed, and we are beloved. Our search for significance begins and ends with our Savior.

KINGDOM THOUGHT 21: DON'T BE SURPRISED

Beloved, do not be surprised at the fiery trial when it comes upon you to test you, as though something strange were happening to you. But rejoice insofar as you share Christ's sufferings, that you may also rejoice and be glad when His glory is revealed.
1 Peter 4:12-13 ESV

Our lives can be full of challenges that often confuse. Many of us have friends and loved ones who are conduits of compassion yet suffer with struggling situations. Some have debilitating health issues . . . some face injustice . . . some live with the consequences of other's decisions.

This life has real suffering and pain. Why can't we walk in heavenly joy instead of wallowing in this hellish junk? Why doesn't God just give us our promised hope, so we aren't grasping for persevering help?

Peter gives us a different perspective for our problems. Often, our understanding is limited. But our God's understanding is limitless. He longs to replace our fear, failure and fatigue with faith.

Our Growth. Peter reminds us to be ready and *"not be surprised at the fiery trial when it comes upon [us] to test [us]"*. Our first response to any difficulty is often surprise and shock. We ask, "How could God allow this to happen?" or "What sin have I committed and why is God punishing me?" Be assured of Paul's encouragement to the Christ-followers in Rome, *"There is no therefore no condemnation to those who are in Christ Jesus"*. (Rom 8:1 ESV). We often see problems as God's punishment, when in reality they are His process in accomplishing His purposes. Peter tells us, *"So if you are suffering in a manner that pleases God, keep on doing what is right, and trust your lives to the God who created you, for He will never fail you."* (1 Pet 4:19 NLT). We don't just sit back and groan in God's decision for us, we stand up grow in God's destiny for us.

His Grace. In our struggles, in our challenges, and even in our weaknesses, He is always there with grace that is perfectly portioned to our pain. Paul encourages us through his own experience, *". . . I was given a thorn in my flesh, a messenger from Satan to torment me and keep me from becoming proud. Three different times I begged the Lord to take it away. Each time He said, 'My grace is all you need. My power works best in weakness.' So now I am glad to boast about my weaknesses, so that the power of Christ can work through me"*. (2 Cor 12:7-9 NLT). Grace is always there . . . we give ourselves to it and go with it. Alexander Whyte writes, "Grace, then, is grace, that is to say, it is sovereign, it is free, it is sure, it is unconditional, and it is everlasting."[33]

His Glory. The apostle Peter's words ring true, *"But rejoice insofar as you share Christ's sufferings, that you may also rejoice and be glad when His glory is revealed."* Sadly, we usually live our lives as if it's all about us . . . our pleasures, our possessions, our performance or our position. That's part of the "keeping ourselves on the throne" struggle. It's really all about Him. Paul gives some insightful instruction, *"That is why we never give up. Though our bodies are dying, our spirits are being renewed every day. For our present troubles are small and won't last very long. Yet they produce for us a glory that vastly outweighs them and will last forever! So we don't look at the troubles we can see now; rather, we fix our gaze on things that cannot be seen. For the things we see now will soon be gone, but the things we cannot see will last forever."* (2 Cor 4:16-18 NLT) Our story is about His glory.

Struggling? Suffering? Sinking? Reach out to the One who has suffered for you and is suffering with you.

His grace is sufficient.

His glory will be seen.

And, our growth will be sure.

KINGDOM THOUGHT 22: TRUST THE PROCESS

Don't be misled: no one makes a fool of God. What a person plants, he will harvest. The person who plants selfishness, ignoring the needs of others—ignoring God—harvests a crop of weeds. All he'll have to show for his life is weeds! But the one who plants in response to God, letting God's Spirit do the growth work in him, harvests a crop of real life, eternal life.
Galatians 6:7-8 MSG

My wife grew up in South Jersey. Her family enjoys farming and for years has produced vegetables for major companies. I have always been amazed how such a vast project begins with a small, simple seed.

We spend our lives harvesting produce from the seeds we plant, fertilize and water. And, the process never fails . . . if you plant a kernel of corn, you'll harvest corn. It's always the same . . . "What a person plants, he will harvest".

Plant The Seeds. The prophet Hosea writes, *"Plant the good seeds of righteousness, and you will harvest a crop of love. Plow up the hard ground of your hearts, for now is the time to seek the Lord, that He may come and shower righteousness upon you."* (Hosea 10:12 NLT). We are all given "seeds to sow" . . . and those seeds are planted in the rich fields of our lives and the lives of others. Although they start out small, they produce a harvest that far exceeds the initial seed. Paul warns the Galatians of those *"who plant selfishness, ignoring the needs of others—ignoring God—harvesting a crop of weeds."* (Gal 6:7). He gives catalytic advice that mirrors the words of Hosea, *"But the one who plants in response to God, letting God's Spirit do the growth work in him, harvests a crop of real life, eternal life."* (Gal 6:8).

Plant right.

Trust The Process. Paul cautions us to not be misled or deceived, *"No one makes a fool of God. What a person plants, he will harvest."* (Gal 6:7). There are not too many "sure things" in life . . . but, this is one. We plant, others water and God gives the increase. Too often, we try to "genetically modify" a process that is contrary to God's. Trust Him. Trust His timing. Trust His process. In his letter to the Christ-followers in Corinth Paul writes, *"Remember this—a farmer who plants only a few seeds will get a small crop. But the one who plants generously will get a generous crop."* (2 Cor 9:6 NLT). Plant seeds every day and trust the process of God's harvest.

Plant well.

Share The Produce. Have you ever asked, "How much is enough"? The harvest that God produces in our lives is not to be selfishly hoarded, but shared. Paul encourages the believers in Corinth, *"You must each decide in your heart how much to give. And, don't give reluctantly or in response to pressure. 'For God loves a person who gives cheerfully.' And God will generously provide all you need. Then you will always have everything you need and plenty left over to share with others."* (2 Cor 9:7-8 NLT). Live with an "open hand". As God gives . . . give . . . it may be giving forward or giving back.

Give freely.

Solomon takes a few words to share insightful wisdom. He writes, *"The fruit of the righteous is a tree of life, and whoever captures souls is wise."* (Prov 11:30 ESV)

Find a moment today to plant seeds of life . . . trust the process . . . and, enjoy the harvest of sharing life with others.

KINGDOM THOUGHT 23: HOW TO LIVE

My old self has been crucified with Christ. It is no longer I who live, but Christ lives in me. So, I live in this earthly body by trusting in the Son of God, who loved me and gave Himself for me.
Galatians 2:20 NLT

Over a half century ago, Francis Schaeffer asked the heart probing question, "How shall we then live?" Schaeffer proposed that establishing a society on the infinite, personal God who speaks, provides an absolute by which we can live. He called this "freedom without chaos".[34]

In Paul's letter to the Christ-followers in Galatia, he underscores the freedom we gain by setting aside self and living in an abiding and loving surrender to Christ. This concept revalues the worth of who we are and redefines the why of our existence. Through Christ and in Christ, we know how we shall live.

Live With Purpose. The Westminster Shorter Catechism states, "Man's chief end is to glorify God and enjoy Him forever".[35] Well known author and pastor, Rick Warren defines a purpose driven life as one of worship, fellowship, discipleship, ministry and mission. These are summed up in the Great Commandment and the Great Commission. We are to *"love the Lord our God with all our heart, all our soul, all our strength, and all our mind"* and, *"love our neighbor as ourselves."* (Luke 10:27 NLT). And, we are to build His Kingdom. Jesus said we are to *"go and make disciples of all the nations."* (Matt 28:19 NLT)

Live With Passion. Oscar Wilde says, "To live is the rarest thing in the world. Most people exist, that is all."[36] Living a life of comfort and complacency can be a life of compromise. Most people desire the exhilaration of the mountain-top experience. Yet, true passion is discovered and determined in the valleys of our lives. Paul clarifies his passion to Christ followers in Philippi, *"I want to know Christ and experience the mighty power that raised Him from the dead. I want to suffer with Him, sharing in His death."* (Phil 3:10 NLT)

Live With Peace. A surrendered life secures our peace. We have peace for all eternity, and we have peace in our every day. Paul writes, *"Therefore, since we have been made right in God's sight by faith, we have peace with God because of what Jesus Christ our Lord has done for us."* (Rom 5:1 NLT) And, Jesus tells us, *"I am leaving you with a gift—peace of mind and heart. And the peace I give is a gift the world cannot give. So don't be troubled or afraid."* (John 14:27 NLT)

Live With Promise. There's an old song of the faith that says, "This world is not my home, I'm just a passing through. My treasures are laid up somewhere beyond the blue."[37] The promise of Heaven gives us a purpose with hope. Paul writes encouraging words to the discouraged, "*For the Lord Himself will come down from heaven, with a loud command, with the voice of the archangel and with the trumpet call of God, and the dead in Christ will rise first. After that, we who are still alive and are left will be caught up together with them in the clouds to meet the Lord in the air. And so we will be with the Lord forever. Therefore encourage one another with these words.*" (1 Thess 4:16-18 NIV). We have a promised hope.

Our confidence, commitment, and courage are all complete in the crucified Christ.

How then shall we live? With lives defined by purpose, with passion, in peace and with promise only found in our infinite, personal God.

KINGDOM THOUGHT 24: ALL GOOD THINGS

The Lord your God is with you, He is mighty to save. He will take great delight in you, He will quiet you with His love, He will rejoice over you with singing.
Zephaniah 3:17 NIV

There's a saying, "All good things must come to an end." In this almost fatalistic approach to life, the good times are seemingly never going to be long lasting. They are fleeting, short lived and never enough.

The prophet Zephaniah reminds us that God is with us. He is powerful enough to save us from any situation . . . short term and long term. He is passionate enough to love us even when we are under-performing. He enjoys us even when we may not be enjoyable. He soothes us in our sorrow. And, He declares His happiness with us in celebratory song. He gives us good, even in our bad . . . and, His goodness never ends.

These simple four words, *"I am with you"*, are like a secure and strong net, saving us as we fall into despair and discouragement. God's own words remind us of His presence, His promise and His peace.

His Never-Ending Presence. The psalmist writes, *"Yet I am always with you; You hold me by my right hand. You guide me with Your counsel, and afterward You will take me into glory. Whom have I in heaven but You? And earth has nothing I desire besides You. My flesh and my heart may fail, but God is the strength of my heart and my portion forever."* (Ps 73:23–26 NIV). We will always have our ups and downs. But, the presence of God never lets us go so far that He cannot reach us. He is our "evenness" in our extremes. Moses gives us encouraging and exciting insight into Jehovah's care, *"The LORD himself goes before you and will be with you; He will never leave you nor forsake you. Do not be afraid; do not be discouraged."* (Duet 31:8 NIV)

His Never-Ending Promise. Scholars tells us that there are approximately 7,500 promises in God's word.[38] These promises are solely based on the Promise Maker. We never need to wrestle or waver concerning God's commitment in keeping His promises. Paul writes to the Corinthian believers, *"For no matter how many promises God has made, they are 'Yes' in Christ. And so, through Him the 'Amen' is spoken by us to the glory of God."* (2 Cor 1:20 NIV) The promises of God are personalized through persevering faith when we speak "Amen" to them. Our confidence in God allows us to claim His promises.

His Never-Ending Peace. Paul gives us insight into the inseparable link between prayer and peace. He writes to the Christ followers in Philippi, *"Do not* *be anxious about anything, but in every situation, by prayer and petition, with thanksgiving, present your requests to God. And the peace of God, which transcends all understanding, will guard your hearts and your minds in Christ Jesus."* (Phil 4:6-7 NIV).   Jesus assures us of His unique peace. A peace that is different and dynamic, a peace that is not dependent on our surroundings, but on our Sovereign. Jesus reminds us, *"Peace I leave with you; My peace I give you. I do not give to you as the world gives. Do not let your hearts be troubled and do not be afraid."* (John 14:27 NIV).

Love and Outcome recorded a worship song that captures the essence of Zephaniah's words. Read the lyrics of "He Is With Us".[39]

> *"We can trust our God*
> *He knows what He's doing*
> *Though it might hurt now*
> *We won't be ruined*
> *It might seem there's an ocean in between*
> *But He's holding on to you and me*
> *And He's never gonna leave, no*
> *He is with us, He is with us*
> *Always, always*
> *He is with us, He is with us . . . always"*

He presence is never ending. His promises are never broken. His peace will never be taken away. He is with you.

KINGDOM THOUGHT 25: IT'S WORK

So let's not get tired of doing what is good. At just the right time we will reap a harvest of blessing if we don't give up.
Galatians 6:9 NLT

I love to cook. There are still many nights when our family will join forces in the kitchen and share the good times of good fun and good food. One of my favorite dishes to make is risotto. It's a rice dish with added herbs and spices that must be cooked slow, low and with constant stirring. If you get too tired and don't "stir the pot" slowly and consistently, you won't get good creamy and tender risotto.

We often get tired of doing what is good because it just wears us down and takes too long to see any benefit. We "give" but we usually get "taken". We help, but we often get hurt.

Paul reminds the Christ-followers of Galatia that their work of planting good seed will produce a good harvest.

A Work Of Purpose. Engaging in "good" provides an example of our "Good God". It's "shining" our light in darkness so others can see the Savior. Matthew records Jesus' words, *"In the same way, let your light shine before others, so that they may see your good works and give glory to your Father who is in Heaven."* (Matt 5:16 ESV). Our "good works" are seen in how we value others with our words, our actions and our instruction. Paul reminds a young pastor, Titus, *"Show yourself in all respects to be a model of good works, and in your teaching show integrity and dignity."* (Titus 2:7 ESV).

Hone into your purpose.

A Work Of Perseverance. Paul cautions us that a natural tendency is to "give up" or to "grow weary". It's safe to say that "doing good" will wear us down and wear us out . . . it will cost us effort and energy. Staying on course may require sacrificing our convenience. The writer of Hebrews gives some insight, *"Do not neglect to do good and to share what you have, for such sacrifices are pleasing to God."* (Heb 13:16 ESV).

Hold on and persevere.

A Work Of Promise. Paul writes, *"At just the right time we will reap a harvest of blessing if we don't give up."* (Gal 6:9). The harvest usually comes in a different season from the planting. It's persevering and being patient for the promise. Humorist Fannie Flagg writes, "Don't give up before the miracle happens."[40] We reminded to keep watching our Winner, *"Keep your eyes on Jesus, who both began and finished this race we're in. Study how he did it.*

Because he never lost sight of where he was headed—that exhilarating finish in and with God—he could put up with anything along the way: Cross, shame, whatever." (Hebrews 12:2 MSG). Norman Vincent Peale says, "It's always too soon to quit".[41]

Hang on for the promise.

A wise Jewish pastor pens these words, "And let us consider how to stir up one another to love and good works." (Heb 10:24 ESV)

Let's find a way to "stir the pot" of good words, good works and a good walk. These are the seeds for a great harvest.

KINGDOM THOUGHT 26: THE VOICE

The doorkeeper opens it for him, and the sheep hear his voice. He calls his own sheep by name and leads them out.
John 10:3 HCSB

Every day, we hear voices crying out for our attention and affection. Some we recognize as old vices and some as new voices, each trying to capture our thoughts. The noise can be deafening and distracting. Young writes, "Many voices vie for control of your mind, especially when you sit in silence. Many run around in circles, trying to obey the various voices directing their lives. This results in fragmented, frustrating patterns of living."[42]

Jesus describes Himself as a "Good Shepherd" . . . One who's voice is known by his flock.

God speaks to us in our deepest need, calming our deepest fear, comforting our deepest sorrow and soothing our deepest pain.

He speaks with both a still, small voice and with tremendous and thunderous power.

He says just the right thing at just the right time in just the right way.

He speaks with ultimate authority and understanding affection.

We Recognize His Voice. He calls out to the lost, so they be found. (Mark 2:17) He calls with compassion and we answer in confidence. Jesus reminds us, *"After he has gathered his own flock, he walks ahead of them, and they follow him because they know his voice. They won't follow a stranger; they will run from him because they don't know his voice."* (John 10:4-5 NLT)

We Respect His Voice. The psalmist reminds us of the complete authority of God's voice. He writes, *"The voice of the Lord is powerful; the voice of the Lord is full of majesty."* (Ps 29:4 ESV). The omnipotence of His voice commands our obedience. *"The voice of the Lord is over the waters; the God of glory thunders, the Lord, over many waters."* (Ps 29:3 ESV). When He speaks, we listen.

We Rest In His Voice. The psalmist describes The Lord's control over chaos and calm, "For He commanded and raised the stormy wind, which lifted up the waves of the sea . . . He made the storm be still, and the waves of the sea were hushed." (Ps 107:25, 29 ESV) Mark records Jesus' decisive words in the presence of danger, "When Jesus woke up, He rebuked the wind and said to the waves, 'Silence! Be still!' Suddenly the wind stopped, and there was a great calm." (Mark 4:39 NLT). He is there in our chaos to speak words of comfort.

We Respond To His Voice. As a loving Father, He call us, "Or have you forgotten how good parents treat children, and that God regards you as his children? My dear child, don't shrug off God's discipline, but don't be crushed by it either. It's the child he loves that he disciplines; the child he embraces, he also corrects." (Heb 12:4-5 MSG). God never speaks to hurt or harm . . . but to help and encourage.

The enemy speaks with a voice of untruth to confuse, condemn, and corrupt.

God speaks with a voice of truth with clarity, confirmation and comfort.

Casting Crowns reminds us of God's voice of authority and assurance.

> *"But the voice of truth tells me a different story.*
> *The voice of truth says, 'Do not be afraid!'*
> *The voice of truth says, 'This is for My glory'.*
> *Out of all the voices calling out to me,*
> *I will choose to listen and believe the voice of truth."*[43]

Take a moment to "tune out" all the voices that are screaming for your attention . . . and "tune in" the Voice that is calling out with affection.

Hear His voice. Hear the voice of truth.

Kingdom Thought 27: No Fear

There is no fear in love. But perfect love drives out fear, because fear has to do with punishment. The one who fears is not made perfect in love.
1 John 4:18 NIV

Why is it so simple for us to accept God's love at the moment of salvation . . . but such a struggle to appreciate His love in times of suffering?

When facing difficulties, we believe solutions reside within our own skills, smarts or strength. Yet, there is always a "doubt" as to whether or not we have the "right stuff" . . . that's when fear breaks down the door and robs our faith.

The ranging storms of our fears can only be subsided when we surrender to God's control and compassion.

John, the apostle identified as the one whom Jesus loved reminds us, *"There is no fear in love"*. (1 John 4:18). He goes a bit further and says, *"perfect love (God's love) drives out fear"*. When our faith is faltering . . . when our trust is tried . . . when our hope is hindered . . . His love drives any fear, doubt or hopelessness.

God's love is perfect because it is based on Who He is . . .

He Is A Passionate God. God's love is eternity changing and eternally unchanging. Paul tells us, *"But because of His great love for us, God, who is rich in mercy, made us alive with Christ even when we were dead in transgressions—it is by grace you have been saved."* (Eph 2:4-5 NIV). And, in his letter to the believers in Rome, Paul assures us of the permanence of God's passion, *"No power in the sky above or in the earth below—indeed, nothing in all creation will ever be able to separate us from the love of God that is revealed in Christ Jesus our Lord."* (Rom 8:39 NLT)

He Is A Personal God. The psalmist reveals God's consideration of us, *"How precious are Your thoughts about me, O God. They cannot be numbered! I can't even count them; they outnumber the grains of sand! And when I wake up, You are still with me!"* (Ps 139:17-18 NLT). It could be said that we "are always on His mind".

He Is A Patient God. We surrender to the patience of God's tender love. The psalmist reveals God's heart, *"But you, O Lord, are a God of compassion and mercy, slow to get angry and filled with unfailing love and faithfulness."* (Ps 86:15 NLT)

He Is A Pleased God. I grew up with the teaching that success was the sign of God's blessing and struggling was the sign of God's punishment. I remember questioning if God was displeased with me and punishing me every time, I had a setback, suffered loss or got a dent in my car. Paul tells us, *"There is now no more condemnation to those who are in Christ Jesus"*. (Rom 8:1 NIV). God is pleased with me . . . with you . . . with us because of the sacrifice of a Jesus, alone. His love for us is not based on performance and does not have punishment.

He Is A Planning God. The prophet Jeremiah records another aspect of God's love, *"'For I know the plans I have for you,' says the Lord. 'They are plans for good and not for disaster, to give you a future and a hope.'"* (Jer 29:11 NLT). Our God designs each detail of our destiny according to His delight.

Take a moment a recognize His love for you . . . let it define you, let it delight you and let it deliver you.

KINGDOM THOUGHT 28: DEVOTION

Devote yourselves to prayer, being watchful and thankful.
Colossians 4:2

Devotion is defined as a "commitment to a fundamental and primary purpose."

Samuel Chadwick, a 19th century Wesleyan Methodist minister writes, "Prayer is the acid test of devotion".[44] Our devotion to prayer mirrors our dependence on God. It is purpose and passion wrapped in petition. Bunyan reminds us, "Prayer is a shield to the soul, a sacrifice to God, and a scourge for Satan."[45]

Paul encourages the believers in Colossae to let prayer capture their heart. It is to be a "fundamental and primary purpose". Prayer is the fulcrum . . . the point from which all things pivot . . . in our lives. And, in praying, he gives two increasingly important insights.

Be Attentive. Distractions can detour us from the delight of our destiny. The pressing issues of pseudo importance can impact our priority and render us impotent. News Anchor Diane Sawyer posted, "I think the one lesson I have learned is that there is no substitute for paying attention."[46] God longs for us to be attentive to His leading. He desires that we listen to His still small voice, hold unto His helping hand and follow His guiding direction. The psalmist makes his own plea, *"Make me to know Your ways, O Lord; teach me your paths. Lead me in Your truth and teach me, for You are the God of my salvation; for You I wait all the day long."* (Ps 25:4-5). Praying attentively is paying attention.

Be Appreciative. Paul reminds those who walk by faith, *"In everything give thanks; for this is the will of God in Christ Jesus for you."* (1 Thess 5:18 NKJV). When we are able to express appreciation for who we are, where we are, what we have and what have gone through . . . we shift our focus from our burdens to His blessings. Giving thanks guards our thinking from negative traps. Paul writes these enlightening words to the Christ-followers in Philippi, *"Don't worry about anything; instead, pray about everything. Tell God what you need and thank Him for all He has done. Then you will experience God's peace, which exceeds anything we can understand. His peace will guard your hearts and minds as you live in Christ Jesus."* (Phil 4:6-7 NLT). God's promised peace will guard and secure our hearts or what we feel . . . and our minds, what we think.

What will capture our devotion, today?

Criticizing or celebrating?

Discouragement or encouragement.

Tearing down or building up?

Give attention to God's presence and lift your heart with appreciation for His peace and power. Be devoted and He will be our "fundamental and primary purpose".

KINGDOM THOUGHT 29: WORK & WORSHIP

Work willingly at whatever you do, as though you were working for the Lord rather than for people. Remember that the Lord will give you an inheritance as your reward, and that the Master you are serving is Christ.
Colossians 3:23-24 NLT

Reality shows are a media mainstay. Several years ago, one captured my attention. The program, "Undercover Boss" followed an owner of a company as they worked in disguise within their own business. Some situations caused anxiety, while others provided a sense of approval. The clandestine boss was able to see the character and quality of employees from an "up close" and "first-hand" perspective.

A while back, long-time friend and great thinker Matt Willmington shared some insights, "a Christ-follower doesn't sit idle at work. They don't say, 'There's nothing to do.', 'I don't like the work and it's not in my skill set.' or 'I don't know what my boss wants me to do.'" He continues, "Ask for more, do more, dream about ways to improve your task or assignment. Always leave it better than you found it."[47]

In a recent "Work As Worship" Simulcast, Liz Bohannon gave clarity to finding passion, "Our passions are not found in our dreaming . . . Our passions are discovered in our doing".[48]

Paul reminds the Colossian of God's perspective of work for the believer . . . we *"work willingly at whatever we do"*. (Col 3:23) Our willingness originates from our work's Master and our work's meaning.

The Real Boss. Paul clearly defines the real Boss. We are to work "as though you were working for The Lord rather than people". Tim Keller reminds us, "If our identity is in our work, rather than Christ, success will go to our heads, and failure will go to our hearts."[49] In his letter to a young disciple, Paul coaches Timothy with the following instruction, *"This is why we work hard and continue to struggle, for our hope is in the living God, who is the Savior of all people and particularly of all believers."* (1 Tim 4:10 NLT) Remember that *"the Master we are serving is Christ"*. (Col 3:24 NLT)

The Real Business. What we do at work and how we do it is not for our notoriety, but for God's . . . It's not building our kingdom, but His Kingdom . . . It's not for our glory, but for His glory. Paul writes, *"So whether you eat or drink, or whatever you do, do it all for the glory of God."* (1 Cor 10:31 NLT). There must be a divine meaning for our daily mission. Paul continues by describing the desire of his duties, *"I, too, try to please everyone in everything I do. I don't just do what is best for me; I do what is best for others so that many may be saved."* (1 Cor 10:33 NLT). Scottish author and poet, George MacDonald writes, "It is our best work that God wants, not the dregs of our exhaustion. I think he must prefer quality to quantity."[50] Our work habits and work ethics are to reflect His workmanship.

The Real Blessing. A strong work ethic not only provides us with an everyday blessing, but an eternal one, as well. In Eugene Peterson's The Message, he gives some additional thoughts, be *"confident that you'll get paid in full when you come into your inheritance . . . The sullen servant who does shoddy work will be held responsible. Being a follower of Jesus doesn't cover up bad work."* (Col 3:24-25 MSG). Solomon writes, *"Work brings profit, but mere talk leads to poverty!"* (Prov 14:23 NLT) Paul reminds the believers in Corinth, *"Let nothing move you. Always give yourselves fully to the work of the Lord, because you know that your labor in the Lord is not in vain."* (1 Cor 15:58 NIV)

Paul encourages the followers in Colossae, "And whatever you do or say, do it as a representative of the Lord Jesus, giving thanks through him to God the Father." (Col 3:17 NLT).

Patrick Lai with Business As Mission reminds us, "God receives work as worship done unto Him. Put simply: work is worship."[51]

Don't be defined by your work . . . let your work be defined by you.

Kingdom Thought 30: Peace

God blesses those who work for peace, for they will be called the children of God.
Matthew 5:9 NLT

Since 1901, The Nobel Peace Prize has been awarded annually (with some exceptions) to those who have "done the most or the best work for fraternity between nations, for the abolition or reduction of standing armies and for the holding and promotion of peace congresses."[52]

In His teaching about the characteristics of the Kingdom of God, Jesus identifies those who work for peace . . . or peacemakers . . . as the *"children of God"*. Being a peacemaker requires intent and initiative. It is proactive, not passive. It is decisive, not divisive. Paul reminds us that an evidence of God's Spirit residing and abiding in us is peace. (Gal 5:22)

God not only allows us to experience His peace, but to also exemplify His peace. We have the confidence of His peace and we share the comfort of His peace with others. Working for peace is synonymous with walking in love. As recipients of God's love, *"we surely ought to love each other."* (1 John 4:11 NLT). We are known as God's disciples because we "love one another" and we are known as the children of God because we "work for peace".

We Practice Peace. Enjoying God's presence and encouraging God's peace are evidences of His love. In finishing his letter to the Christ-followers in Corinth, Paul writes, *"Dear brothers and sisters, I close my letter with these last words: Be joyful. Grow to maturity. Encourage each other. Live in harmony and peace. Then the God of love and peace will be with you."* (2 Cor 13:11 NLT)

We Promote Peace. Jesus parallels the seasoning with salt with the promotion of peace. Mark records His words, *"Salt is good for seasoning. But if it loses its flavor, how do you make it salty again? You must have the qualities of salt among yourselves and live in peace with each other."* (Mark 9:50 NLT) Making peace becomes our marketing brand. Our promotion of peace leads others to the Prince of Peace.

We Pursue Peace. We go after peace with passionate pursuit. It's a characteristic of our Kingdom citizenship. Paul writes to the believers in Rome, *"For the kingdom of God is not a matter of eating and drinking but of righteousness and peace and joy in the Holy Spirit. Whoever thus serves Christ is acceptable to God and approved by men. So then let us pursue what makes for peace and for mutual upbuilding."* (Romans 14:17-19 ESV)

Two influential women provide some introspective thoughts on peace. Eleanor Roosevelt says, "It isn't enough to talk about peace, one must believe it. And it isn't enough to believe in it, one must work for it."[53] We can make the first step of making peace with a simple expression. Mother Teresa comments, "A smile is the beginning of peace."[54]

Make peace a part of your purpose . . . and, let your smile be an invitation to harmony.

KINGDOM THOUGHT 31: A GOOD MYSTERY

This mystery has been kept in the dark for a long time, but now it's out in the open. God wanted everyone, not just Jews, to know this rich and glorious secret inside and out, regardless of their background, regardless of their religious standing. The mystery in a nutshell is just this: Christ is in you, so therefore you can look forward to sharing in God's glory. It's that simple.
Colossians 1:26-27 MSG

One of most popular genres of literature is mystery. The suspense . . . the intrigue . . . the woven story lines. Each lead us down a path of supposition only to be surprised.

Throughout God's relationship with man, He surprises us. His mystery was hidden for ages but is now revealed. It's the greatest mystery of all time.

We grieve for a better or meaningful life and He gives us both . . . we can't earn it, work for it, qualify for it, or aren't good enough for it. He just gives it to us . . . He gives us hope that is every day and for all eternity. Paul tells us, *"God saved you by His grace when you believed. And you can't take credit for this; it is a gift from God. Salvation is not a reward for the good things we have done, so none of us can boast about it."* (Eph 2:8-9 NLT)

God's Affection. We are unloved, unworthy and unaccepted . . . God gives us love, value and acceptance. His love is deep, decisive and dedicated. His love is grounded in Who He is and not in what we do. The apostle John writes, *"This is real love—not that we loved God, but that he loved us and sent his Son as a sacrifice to take away our sins."* (1 John 4:10 NLT)

God's Approval. We don't have to prove ourselves . . . He's already proven His love. We don't have to be better . . . He's already made us better than we can be. Paul tells the hopeful in Ephesus, *"For we are God's masterpiece. He has created us anew in Christ Jesus, so we can do the good things he planned for us long ago."* (Eph 2:10 NLT)

God's Acceptance. We don't have to work at changing . . . He's already doing the work of changing us inside. Paul writes to believers in Philippi, *"And I am certain that God, Who began the good work within you, will continue his work until it is finally finished on the day when Christ Jesus returns."* (Phil 1:6 NLT)

And, there's more to the mystery . . .

He gives joy without judgement.

He gives peace without pressure.

He gives encouragement without evaluation.

He gives liberty without law.

He gives belonging without burden.

He gives acceptance without any attachments.

God living in me. I can't understand it . . . never will.

It's like every good mystery . . . when it's revealed, the only thing you can say is, "Wow. I didn't see that coming."

KINGDOM THOUGHT 32: MOMENT MIRACLES

Give unto the LORD the glory due to His name; Worship the LORD in the beauty of holiness.
Psalms 29:2 NKJV

We like the "big" miracles of God: the dramatic conversion, the restoration of a ruined family, or the healing of a hopeless situation. These show us the powerful hand of God. They illustrate His greatness.

We live amid the "small" moments of God: the beauty of a rose, the daily majesty of a brilliant sunset, the trusting smile of a child. These show us the prominent fingerprint of God. They illuminate His glory.

One of the challenges we face is getting caught up in the daily tasks of life. We keep our nose to the proverbial grindstone and never look up to see God's glory. Our routines can become ruts. But when we set aside the routine of the mundane, we are able recognize the majestic.

See His Glory. We often hear a common saying, "Give credit where credit is due". It simply means recognition goes to the rightful source. John reminds us of a time when Christ will rule during His Kingdom and all will give Him honor, glory and praise. He writes, *"You are worthy, O Lord our God, to receive glory and honor and power. For you created all things, and they exist because you created what You pleased."* (Rev 4:11 NLT). Take a moment to look around . . . the dawning of the day . . . the carefree spirit of a child . . . the playfulness of a pet . . . the individuality of individuals. His artistry is seen in His masterpieces. His creation cries out with His creativity.

Look around and see His glory.

See His Grace. Grace impacts our eternity and our everyday. God's grace redeems us . . . and, His grace reminds us. Paul tells the believers in Ephesus, *"God saved you by His grace when you believed . . . For we are God's masterpiece. He has created us anew in Christ Jesus, so we can do the good things he planned for us long ago."* (Eph 2:8-10 NLT). We experience His grace in our own transformation and we express His grace in our testimony to others of His love. Redemption leads to reconciliation. The apostle writes, *"And all of this is a gift from God, who brought us back to himself through Christ. And God has given us this task of reconciling people to Him."* (2 Cor 5:18 NLT).

Look around and see His grace.

See His Gifts. Awesome gift givers give amazing gifts. James tells us, *"Every good and perfect gift is from above, coming down from the Father of the heavenly lights, who does not change like shifting shadows."* (James 1:17 NIV).

Take another look at Paul's explanation of grace, "For it is by free grace that you are saved through your faith. And this is not of your own doing, it came not through your own striving, but it is the gift of God." (Eph 2:8 AMP). Our eternal life is a *"free gift of God through Jesus"*. (Rom 6:23 ESV). Grace grants us family access and acceptance. God is a giving and gracious Father. Solomon reminds us that our own children are an awesome blessing. He writes, *"Children are a gift from the LORD; they are a reward from Him."* (Ps 127:3 NLT). What amazing gifts . . . faith, future, friends, family . . . what an amazing gift Giver.

Look around and see His gifts.

Take time to "smell the roses" and you will see the Redeemer.

Ponder His gifts and you will promote His glory.

Enjoy His everyday creation and you will experience the Everlasting Creator.

Appreciate your incredible family and you will acknowledge our indescribable Father.

The beauty of His holiness is a breathtaking view. His fingerprints can be seen everywhere.

Give Him the praise He is due. Our God is an awesome God.

KINGDOM THOUGHT 33: DEEPEST NEED

O God, you are my God; I earnestly search for you. My soul thirsts for You; my whole-body longs for You in this parched and weary land where there is no water.
Psalms 63:1 NLT

The rat-race and fast-pace of religious exercises can lead to real emptiness. Lance Witt writes, "You can't live at warp speed without warping your soul".[55] The warp speed of our journey may need to give way to a walking stroll with Jesus.

David composes this worship song in the setting of rugged wilderness, not while serving in religious worship. The psalmist identifies a thirst that cannot be quickly quenched and a hunger that will not be satisfied with a snack.

Swindoll writes, "Most likely on the run from Saul, David found himself alone, removed, obscure, separated from every comfort and friend, acutely feeling the effects of thirst, hunger, pain, loneliness, and exhaustion. Even so, he didn't regard these as his most pressing needs. He identifies his deepest need."[56]

It wasn't the most "pressing need", but the "deepest need".

He Is Our Savior. Unashamedly and unreservedly, the psalmist claims God as his own. There is a confidence that rises up within us when there is a conviction that our relationship with God is secure. God chose us before the foundations of the world and free of any influence we may want to give. The choice is His. Hillsong writes the following lyrics, *" You are my King, You are my God. The praises I bring come from my heart."* Because God decides that we are His, we can declare that He is our God. Isaiah reminds us, *"O LORD, You are my God; I will exalt You, I will give thanks to Your name; For You have worked wonders, plans formed long ago, with perfect faithfulness."* (Is 25:1 ESV)

He Is Our Search. God is the motivation that gets us up in the morning. He is the message on our hearts. He is the moving force in our soul. He is the meaning of our life. The prophet Isaiah writes, *"My soul yearns for you in the night; in the morning my spirit longs for you. When your judgments come upon the earth, the people of the world learn righteousness."* (Is 26:9 NIV). When we search for Him, we will find Him. And, when we find Him, we find our purpose. Amos tells the nation, *"Thus says the Lord to Israel: 'Seek me and live.'"* (Amos 5:4 ESV)

He Is Our Satisfaction. There's an old hymn that says, "Only Jesus can satisfy my soul". When we come to His table, He fills us up. Jesus reminds us, *"Blessed are those who hunger and thirst for righteousness, for they will be filled."* (Matt

5:6 NIV). Our God gives us rest and refreshment. Jeremiah writes, *"I will refresh the weary and satisfy the faint."* (Jer 31:25 NIV) Our search for Him is always satisfied.

When today's weariness wears you out and its dryness drains you. Find renewal and refreshment in Jesus.

He is the Well that never runs dry and the Spring that always satisfies.

KINGDOM THOUGHT 34: TURN AROUNDS

Only fools say in their hearts, "There is no God." They are corrupt, and their actions are evil; not one of them does good!
Psalms 14:1 NLT

My Father-in-law always loved sharing jokes on "April Fool's Day". He would get a twinkle in his eye while having fun with others.

There is another kind of fool. It's not one who delights in joking but, one who denies the power, passion, purpose and presence of God.

As God considers His creation, He finds none who are righteous, none who are good, and all have fallen short. There is no hope . . . we are all broken . . . and we are all lost. Paul captures this sentiment in his letter to the church of Rome, *"No one is righteous— not even one. No one is truly wise; no one is seeking God. All have turned away; all have become useless. No one does good, not a single one."* (Rom 3:10-12 NLT). The psalmist writes, *"The Lord looks down from heaven on the children of man, to see if there are any who understand, who seek after God."* (Ps 14:2 NLT)

At some point, we all are hopeless, in need of encouragement. We are broken, in need of fixing. We are lost, in need of rescuing.

"Turn arounds" are fascinating. A "turn around" occurs when hope is restored, brokenness is rebuilt, or purpose is renewed. David, the shepherd king reminds us of our only Solution, *"Is there anyone around to save Israel? Yes. God is around; God turns life around . . . "* (Ps 14:7 MSG)

God turns lives around, He is ready, willing and able to do the same to all who respond to the Savior.

His Unending Mercy. God's mercy gives us great help and great hope. Peter tells us, "All praise to God, the Father of our Lord Jesus Christ. It is by his great mercy that we have been born again, because God raised Jesus Christ from the dead. Now we live with great expectation." (1 Pet 1:3 NLT)

This is the power of God.

His Unfailing Love. The psalmist writes, *"O Lord, you are so good, so ready to forgive, so full of unfailing love for all who ask for your help."* (Psalms 86:5 NLT). God, is love . . . just as He has no beginning or no end, so His love is the same.

This is the passion of God.

His Unlimited Grace. Mercy and love partner to display God's grace. Paul tells us, "But God is so rich in mercy, and He loved us so much, that even though we were dead because of our sins, He gave us life when he raised Christ from the dead. (It is only by God's grace that you have been saved!) . . . God saved you by His grace when you believed. And you can't take credit for this; it is a gift from God." (Eph 2:4-5, 8 NLT)

This is the purpose of God.

Is there anyone Who can restore, rebuild and renew? Yes!!! It's God and He turns lives around.

It's a good day for a turn around. No fooling . . .

Kingdom Thought 35: Someday

Then, together with them, we who are still alive and remain on the earth will be caught up in the clouds to meet the Lord in the air. Then we will be with the Lord forever. So, encourage each other with these words.
1 Thessalonians 4:17-18 NLT

In 1978, Peaches & Herb recorded a hit song with the chorus, "Reunited and it feels so good". Although they captured the sentiment of lost love, they most likely missed the reality of a returning Lord. We're reminded that our Redeemer will return. And, when He does, we will experience a newness in healing, hope and our home.

Paul implores us to "encourage each other with these words" . . . Jesus is returning, and we will be reunited . . . and it will be good.

Healing. The infirmities, fragility and weaknesses that plague us in this life pass away in the life to come. John writes, *"He will wipe away every tear from their eyes, and death shall be no more, neither shall there be mourning, nor crying, nor pain anymore, for the former things have passed away."* (Rev 21:4 ESV). Our new bodies will be crafted by our Creator. Paul reminds us, *"For we know that when this earthly tent we live in is taken down (that is, when we die and leave this earthly body), we will have a house in heaven, an eternal body made for us by God himself and not by human hands."* (2 Cor 5:1 NLT).

Hope. C. S. Lewis writes, "No one ever told me that grief felt so like fear."[57] The loneliness of loss can produce a traumatic terror. Our faith, partnered with love, battles the fear in our lives. Fear of failure, fear of loss, fear of abandonment . . . are all displaced with the faith that produces hope and love. The believers in Rome are encouraged, *"And this hope will not lead to disappointment. For we know how dearly God loves us, because He has given us the Holy Spirit to fill our hearts with his love."* (Romans 5:5 NLT). Through Christ, we have help for today and hope for tomorrow.

Heaven. The old chorus reminds us, "Heaven is a wonderful place, filled with glory and grace."[58] This life is a steppingstone to a secured eternity. Eugene Peterson, in The Message, captures Paul encouraging words to Christ-followers in Philippi, *"But there's far more to life for us. We're citizens of high heaven! We're waiting the arrival of the Savior, the Master, Jesus Christ, who will transform our earthy bodies into glorious bodies like his own. He'll make us beautiful and whole with the same powerful skill by which he is putting everything as it should be, under and around him."* (Phil 3:20-21 MSG) Some say Heaven is a crutch . . . to those who know Christ it is a commitment . . . a commitment of new healing, new hope and a new home. John records Jesus promised words, *"And the One sitting on the throne said, 'Look, I am making everything new!' And then He said to me, 'Write this down, for what I tell you is trustworthy and true.'"* (Rev 21:5 NLT)

Someone once said, "Goodbyes are not forever. Goodbyes are not the end. They simply mean I'll miss you until we meet again!" Our faith means we will be with our Savior, and those who have trusted in Him . . . FOREVER.

Today is a day to be encouraged.

New healing . . . new hope . . . new home . . . Heaven.

Kingdom Thought 36: He Is

God arms me with strength, and He makes my way perfect.
Psalms 18:32 NLT

There are a lot of days when life seems imperfect.

It feels like the "UN-life" . . . unmet expectations, unfulfilled dreams, unresolved issues and unpaid bills. Any hope is consumed by overwhelming hopelessness and any faith is corrupted by overshadowing fear.

It's in those times of upheaval that God reaches down.

Paul encourages us with his writings to the Christ-followers in Philippi, *"And I am certain that God, who began the good work within you, will continue his work until it is finally finished on the day when Christ Jesus returns."* (Phil 1:6 NLT) When we are battered, beaten and broken, He renews us with the blessings of His presence, His peace and His promises.

God has not quit. God has not given up. God is not done.

When We Are Weak, He Gives Strength. The psalmist is confident, *"God arms me with strength"*. In our weaknesses, He is always there with power that is perfectly suited for our struggle. Through his own challenges, Paul gives us comfort, *". . . I was given a thorn in my flesh, a messenger from Satan to torment me and keep me from becoming proud. Three different times I begged the Lord to take it away. Each time He said, 'My grace is all you need. My power works best in weakness.' So now I am glad to boast about my weaknesses, so that the power of Christ can work through me"*. (2 Cor 12:7-9 NLT). Paul also reminds those in Philippi, *"For I can do everything through Christ, who gives me strength."* (Phil 4:13 NLT)

When We Are Weary, He Gives Rest. The prophet, Jeremiah declares God's encouraging words to the exhausted nation of Israel . . . *"For I will satisfy the weary soul, and every languishing soul I will replenish."* (Jer 31:25 ESV) He refreshes and replenishes. He fills in and fills up. He satisfies the faint and strengthens the failing. In our exhaustion, He wants us to embrace Him. Jesus tells us, *"Come to me, all of you who are weary and carry heavy burdens, and I will give you rest."* (Matt 11:28 NLT)

When We Are Worn Out, He Gives Renewal. God's brings rejuvenation and restoration through worship and His word. Solomon writes, *"My child, pay attention to what I say. Listen carefully to my words. Don't lose sight of them. Let them penetrate deep into your heart, for they bring life to those who find them, and healing to their whole body."* (Prov 4:20-22 NLT) Never lose sight of God's promises. Remember them, rehearse them and recall them. Drive them into the depths of your heart. Moses reminds us, *"Repeat them again and again to your children. Talk about them when you are at home and when you are on the road, when you are going to bed and when you are getting up."* (Deut 6:7)

When we are Wanting, He Gives Resources. Today, this is one I need to claim by faith. Paul reminds us *"And my God will supply every need of yours according to his riches in glory in Christ Jesus."* (Phil 4:19 ESV) When our provisions are lacking, He is the Provider who loves. Corallie Buchanan writes, "When we look to God as provider, we are surrendering our independence and trusting someone else to meet our needs, over which we have no control."[59] Often the need seems impossible and the solution seems improbable. Chuck Swindoll encourages us, "The size of a challenge should never be measured by what we have to offer. It will never be enough. Furthermore, provision is God's responsibility, not ours. We are merely called to commit what we have - even if it's no more than a sack lunch."[60]

Our God is faithful.

These lyrics from Matt Redman's "Never Once" remind us that God is making our way perfect . . .

> *"Standing on this mountaintop,*
> *Looking just how far we've come,*
> *Knowing that for every step,*
> *You were with us."*
>
> *"Kneeling on this battle ground,*
> *Seeing just how much You've done,*
> *Knowing every victory,*
> *Was Your power in us."*
>
> *"Scars and struggles on the way*
> *But with joy our hearts can say,*
> *Yes, our hearts can say . . . "*
>
> *"Never once did we ever walk alone.*
> *Never once did You leave us on our own.*
> *You are faithful, God, You are faithful."*[61]

Never once . . . not one time.

He is always there; He is faithful, and He always cares.

KINGDOM THOUGHT 37: SEEDS

Do not be deceived. God will not be made a fool. For a person will reap what he sows.
Galatians 6:7 NET

Many make their livelihood with products that begin with a seed. Food, drink, clothing and other enjoyments start with a seed. Dreams and ideas often begin with a "seed" thought . . . something so small can be surprisingly significant.

A friend of mine writes, "The seeds of victory are found in defeat. They are planted by faith. They are watered by commitment. They are weeded and fertilized by persistence. They are harvested by perseverance."[62]

I love the contemplation behind these thoughts. In our days of instantaneous and immediate gratification, we often forget the investment of a grueling growth process.

Solomon reminds us of the regiment of resilience, *"for the righteous falls seven times and rises again".* (Prov 24:16 ESV) Failure is not bad until we refuse to find its blessing. In our learning failures, we fall and get back up. In our losing failures, we fall and never get back up. The seeds of success can be found in the fruit of failure.

Planted By Promise. Seeds are planted with the promise of a harvest. Interestingly, ever planted seed must deteriorate in the ground before new growth can begin. John records the words of Jesus, *"I tell you the truth, unless a kernel of wheat is planted in the soil and dies, it remains alone. But its death will produce many new kernels—a plentiful harvest of new lives."* (John 12:24 NLT). We rarely see the germination part of the process as its buried deep in the soil. The new birth, new life and new growth all require faith . . . and the process of faith is buried deep within our souls. The faith becomes our promise. The writer of Hebrews reminds us, *"Faith is the confidence that what we hope for will actually happen; it gives us assurance about things we cannot see."* (Heb 11:1 NLT)

Watered With Purpose. Watering is a daily process. The germinated seed absorbs nutrients from its surrounding soil. Water moistens the soil and releases more life-giving nutrition, also allowing them to flow throughout the growing plant. Water also provides "turgidity" . . . the process which prevents wilting. Our purpose becomes our turgidity. Intimacy with God and instruction from His word intensify His purpose in our lives. Jesus says, *"Already you are clean because of the word that I have spoken to you."* (John 15:3 ESV)

Weeded With Persistence. Weeds grow. Weeds always grow faster that planted crops. Unless we persistently prune and pull out life-robbing weeds, they will take over our crops. Jesus models this process in our own lives. John reminds us of Jesus' words, *"Every branch in me that does not bear fruit He (God) takes away, and every branch that does bear fruit He prunes, that it may bear more fruit."* (John 15:2 ESV). Many give up on their crop when weeds start to take over. Be persistent.

Harvested By Perseverance. Paul reminds the believers in Galatia, *"So we must not grow weary in doing good, for in due time we will reap, if we do not give up."* (Gal 6:9 NET). David Bly says, "Striving for success without hard work is like trying to harvest where you haven't planted."[63] We can have a part in this "God-process". Paul writes, *"I planted, Apollos watered, but God gave the growth."* (1 Cor 3:6 ESV)

Og Mandino reminds us, "Always do your best. What you plant now, you will harvest later."[64]

Eugene Peterson illustrates the apostle Paul's impacting insight into the planting process, *"Remember: A stingy planter gets a stingy crop; a lavish planter gets a lavish crop. I want each of you to take plenty of time to think it over, and make up your own mind what you will give . . . God loves it when the giver delights in the giving."* (2 Cor 9:6-7 MSG)

We can never out-plant God . . . we can never out-give God.

Trust the growing process.

KINGDOM THOUGHT 38: COMFORT

He comforts us in all our troubles so that we can comfort others. When they are troubled, we will be able to give them the same comfort God has given us.
2 Corinthians 1:4 NLT

It was a tradition every year . . . our pastor would remind us that God is "The God of all encouragement". Teaching from Paul's words, we were given hope in the Holy One . . . The God of Encouragement, The God Who Comforts, The Prince of Peace (Is 9:6)

Ralph Waldo Emerson encourages us, "When it is dark enough, you can see the stars."[65] God lights our life with encouragement even in our darkest experiences.

He Is Comfort. The psalmist lived in the looming love of His Lord. David writes, *"God is our refuge and strength, always ready to help in times of trouble."* (Ps 46:1 NLT). In our struggles we find strength and safety in our Savior. The prophet reminds us, *"The Lord is good, a stronghold in the day of trouble; He knows those who take refuge in Him."* (Nahum 1:7 ESV). Jesus promises us His presence through His Spirit, *"But the Comforter, which is the Holy Ghost, whom the Father will send in My name, He shall teach you all things, and bring all things to your remembrance, whatsoever I have said unto you."* (John 14:26 AMP)

He Gives Comfort. Shakespeare writes, "Now, God be praised, that to believing souls gives light in darkness, comfort in despair." Burdens can be heavy to carry. God wants and waits for us to release the grip on our problems and rest in the grace of His peace. David encourages us, *"Give your burdens to the Lord, and He will take care of you. He will not permit the godly to slip and fall."* (Ps 55:22 NLT). Peace is not only found in God's presence, but also in His promises. God's words of blessing relieve the weight of burden. The psalmist declares, *"This is my comfort in my affliction, that Your promise gives me life."* (Ps 119:50 ESV)

We Share Comfort. We are reminded, *"He [God] comforts us in all our troubles so that we can comfort others."* (2 Cor 1:4 NLT). God gives to us so we can give to others. Some call this "the stewardship of sharing". Paul tells the Christ-followers in Galatia, *"Share each other's burdens, and in this way obey the law of Christ. If you think you are too important to help someone, you are only fooling yourself. You are not that important."* (Gal 6:2, 3 NLT)

God's comfort is just a hint of heavenly joy that awaits us. Missionary Adoniram Judson writes, "Thanks be to God, not—only for 'rivers of endless joys above', but for 'rills of comfort here below.'"[66]

Release the burdens that are hard to carry . . . rest in the comfort that God promises . . . and, respond to others with comfort received.

KINGDOM THOUGHT 39: LOVE AND LEGACY

Write these commandments that I've given you today on your hearts. Get them inside of you and then get them inside your children. Talk about them wherever you are, sitting at home or walking in the street; talk about them from the time you get up in the morning to when you fall into bed at night. Tie them on your hands and foreheads as a reminder; inscribe them on the doorposts of your homes and on your city gates.
Deuteronomy 6:6-9 MSG

Loving God . . . Loving family . . . Loving people.

In this Old Testament passage, the nation of Israel is miraculously freed from bondage and enslavement. As they stand on the precipice of promise, Moses gives them the ground rules, *"Listen, O Israel! The Lord is our God, the Lord alone. And you must love the Lord your God with all your heart, all your soul, and all your strength."* (Deut 6:4-5 NLT). Thousands of years later, Jesus gives a similar answer, *"This is the first and greatest commandment. A second is equally important: 'Love your neighbor as yourself.' The entire law and all the demands of the prophets are based on these two commandments."* (Matt 22:38-40 NLT)

Intimacy with God always impacts others. Moses gives several powerful and practical ways to prioritize these principles.

Learn Them. The process begins by inscribing these mandates "on our hearts". Moses writes, *"Get them inside you and them get them inside your children."* (Deut 6:6 MSG). We engage God's word as those who are not *"ashamed and who correctly explain the word of truth."* (2 Tim 2:15 NLT). Paul tells us God's Word *"is useful to teach us what is true and to make us realize what is wrong in our lives. It corrects us when we are wrong and teaches us to do what is right. God uses it to prepare and equip his people to do every good work."* (2 Tim 3:16, 17 NLT) And, he writes to those in Rome, *"to be transformed by the renewal of your minds."* (Rom 12:2).

This is our investment.

Live Them. It's not enough to learn these truths . . . we must live them. Moses takes the next step, *"Talk about them wherever you are, sitting at home or walking in the street; talk about them from the time you get up in the morning to when you fall into bed at night."* Our devotion becomes our declaration. The psalmist writes, *"O Lord, open my lips, and my mouth will declare your praise."* (Ps 51:15 ESV) Peter reminds us, *"But you are a chosen race, a royal priesthood,* *a holy nation, a people for His own possession, that you may proclaim the excellencies of Him who called you out of darkness into His marvelous light."* (1 Pet 2:9 ESV).

This is our integration.

Leave Them. The investment of God's Word and its integration in our daily lives leaves an eternal imprint on all we encounter. For some, it's Illustrated as *"tying them on your hands and foreheads as a reminder; inscribe them on the doorposts of your homes and on your city gates."* We never concede, we celebrate. Loving God always leads to loving people. Our compassion is our calling card. Our love is a looking glass into the Kingdom. John writes, *"We love because He first loved us."* (1 John 4:19 ESV)

This is our impact.

Dr. Tony Evans writes, "The single greatest reason why we are losing a generation is because the home is no longer the place of transference of the faith. We live in a day of 'outsourcing'."[67]

A friend once encouraged me to "leave it better than you found it". What we learn, God wants us to live and leave with others. Jana Magruder writes in her book, Nothing Less, "People do what they value.".[68]

Learn His Truth. Live it daily. Leave it with others.

Love God . . . Love People . . . Leave a Legacy.

Kingdom Thought 40: The Right Words

For whatever was written in former days was written for our instruction, that through endurance and through the encouragement of the Scriptures we might have hope.
Romans 15:4 ESV

It's been said that history is His Story. God uses the lessons learned and lived by others to teach and guide us in our own lives. His story tells us His truth.

Mother Teresa writes, "Some people come in your life as blessings. Some come in your life as lessons."[69] An insightful mentor once told me, "Wise men learn from the mistakes of others, smart men learn from their own and foolish men never learn". We are reminded that "whatever was written in former days" was written for our benefit and blessing.

The words of learning become words of life.

Words To Educate. Eugene Peterson reminds us of Paul's instruction, *"Every part of Scripture is God-breathed and useful one way or another—showing us truth, exposing our rebellion, correcting our mistakes, training us to live God's way."* (2 Tim 3:16 MSG) The apostle tells us, *"God uses it to prepare and equip his people to do every good work."* (2 Tim 3:17 NLT) God's word is more than a history book or a collection of literary poems, parables or proverbs . . . It is life-giving, life-changing and life-challenging insight from the heart and hand of God.

Words For Endurance. God's principles are the seeds of potential and powerful promises. Paul writes, *"We also pray that you will be strengthened with all His glorious power so you will have all the endurance and patience you need. May you be filled with joy,"* (Col 1:11 NLT). God's insights deepen our faith and trust. His truth provides a tether for our trials. James writes, *"For you know that when your faith is tested, your endurance has a chance to grow. So let it grow, for when your endurance is fully developed, you will be perfect and complete, needing nothing."* (James 1:3-4 NLT)

Words To Encourage. God's word gives us hope and help. It creates purpose and confirms promises. It soothes and strengthens. It edifies and encourages. Peter reminds us, *". . . My purpose in writing is to encourage you and assure you that what you are experiencing is truly part of God's grace for you. Stand firm in this grace."* (1 Pet 5:12 NLT) What God says, He will do. Theologian J.I. Packer instructs, "The stars may fail, but God's promises will stand and be fulfilled."[70]

George Mueller, a man of unshakable faith writes, "Be assured, if you walk with Him and look to Him, and expect help from Him, He will never fail you."[71]

God's word teaches us endurance and encouragement . . . take hold of His Truth and it will never let you go.

KINGDOM THOUGHT 41: JOY

For His anger is but for a moment, and His favor lasts a lifetime. Weeping may last through the night, but joy comes with the morning.
Psalm 30:5 NLT

There is a newness that comes with the beginning of each day. Springtime mornings introduce us to budding of new blossoms. Each dawn brings new light, new beginning and new hope.

The psalmist declares that God's great love replaces our old routine with a new normal. David writes, *"You have turned my wailing into dancing; You have removed my sackcloth and clothed me with joy."* (Ps 30:11 NIV).

His heartache turns to happiness.

His grief transforms to gladness.

We may have the sadness of weeping through the night, but a wonderful joy is ours each and every morning.

The Joy Of His Presence. There is a simple and significant joy that comes from resting in the presence of God. The psalmist reminds us, *"You will show me the way of life, granting me the joy of your presence and the pleasures of living with you forever."* (Ps 16:11 NLT). A. W. Tozer writes, "What I am anxious to see in Christian believers is a beautiful paradox. I want to see in them the joy of finding God while at the same time they are blessedly pursuing Him. I want to see in them the great joy of having God yet always wanting Him."[72] There is joy in sitting at His feet and being surrounded with His presence.

The Joy Of His Peace. There is a inexplicable link between joy and peace. The benefits of trusting and confident hope are provided to us by God's Spirit. Paul writes, *"I pray that God, the source of hope, will fill you completely with joy and peace because you trust in Him. Then you will overflow with confident hope through the power of the Holy Spirit."* (Rom 15:13 NLT). When we trust, He turns our trials into triumphs and gives peace in our problems.

The Joy Of His Promise. C.S. Lewis writes, "Joy is the serious business in Heaven."[73] The teachings of Jesus become the serious truth for our joy. His promise to always be with us produces a joy that is indescribable and full of glory. Jesus encourages his disciples, *"I have told you these things so that you may be filled with My joy. Yes, your joy will overflow."* (John 15:11 NLT). His Word fills us up with His joy.

In 1996, Bill and Gloria Gaither released the following lyrics:

> *"If you've knelt beside the rubble of an aching broken heart,*
> *When the things you gave your life to fell apart.*
> *You're not the first to be acquainted with sorrow, grief or pain,*
> *But the Master promised sunshine after rain."*
> *"Hold on my child joy comes in the morning,*
> *Weeping only last for the night.*
> *Hold on my child Joy comes in the morning,*
> *The darkest hour means dawn is just in sight."*[74]

Buried in all our struggles are treasures of joy.

Expect them.

Experience them.

Embrace them.

Enjoy them.

KINGDOM THOUGHT 42: OVERCOMERS

I have told you all this so that you may have peace in Me. Here on earth you will have many trials and sorrows. But take heart, because I have overcome the world.
John 16:33 NLT

Jesus understands the difficult and demoralizing times that His followers face. Our enemy's objective is to *"kill, steal and destroy"* (John 10:10) our life, our living and our legacy. He uses doubt and disappointment . . . fear and failure . . . struggles and suffering . . . to paralyze and punish us.

Trials and sorrows are part of life on this side of eternity. Jesus encourages us with a *"peace that passes all understanding"* (Phil 4:7) and a presence that will always be with us. (Matt 28:10). There will always be struggles . . . but we always have a Source of strength and security.

Opposition. Life is frail and fragile, easily broken and bruised. The "fairy tale" usually doesn't turn out happily ever after. Heartache and hopelessness happen. James reminds us, *"Dear brothers and sisters, when troubles of any kind come your way, consider it an opportunity for great joy. For you know that when your faith is tested, your endurance has a chance to grow."* (Jam 1:2-3 NLT). It's not "if" they will come . . . but "when" will they come. Expect trouble. Embrace it. Exchange it for joy. And, endure.

Opportunity. Failure is not falling down, it's staying down. Peter tells us, *"So be truly glad. There is wonderful joy ahead, even though you must endure many trials for a little while. These trials will show that your faith is genuine. It is being tested as fire tests and purifies gold—though your faith is far more precious than mere gold."* (1 Pet 1:6-7 NLT). In every difficulty, there is a deliverance. In every painful experience, there is a purposeful explanation. In every obstacle, there is an opportunity. Alexander Graham Bell said, "When one door closes another door opens; but we so often look so long and so regretfully upon the closed door, that we do not see the ones which open for us."[75] Stay focused on the possibility, not in the problem.

Overcoming. We have His peace and we have His promises. John, a fisherman and follower of Jesus reminds us, *"For this is the love of God, that we keep his commandments. And his commandments are not burdensome. For everyone who has been born of God overcomes the world. And this is the victory that has overcome the world— our faith."* (1 John 5:3-4). God's compassion gives us the confidence to be conquerors.

In her song "Overcomer", Mandisa writes these encouraging lyrics,

> *"Whatever it is you may be going through,*
> *I know He's not gonna let it get the best of you.*
> *You're an overcomer*
> *Stay in the fight until the final round.*
> *You're not going under*
> *'Cause God is holding you right now.*
> *You might be down for a moment*
> *Feeling like it's hopeless*
> *That's when He reminds You*
> *That you're an overcomer.*
> *You're an overcomer."*[76]

In your struggles, see your Savior.

In your pain, see your Prince of Peace.

In your troubles, see your Triumphant Truth.

In your obstacles, see your Overcomer.

Eugene Peterson reminds us of Jesus' words, "*The Father is with me. I've told you all this so that trusting me, you will be unshakable and assured, deeply at peace. In this godless world you will continue to experience difficulties. But take heart! I've conquered the world.*" (John 16:32-33 MSG)

We are overcomers through the One who overcomes.

Kingdom Thought 43: I Need A Break

I will fully satisfy the needs of those who are weary and fully refresh the souls of those who are faint.
Jeremiah 31:25 NET

Weary? Worn out? Whipped?

We are always on the go . . . always working . . . always connecting. We give the nod to the novel notion that we are masters of our own lives. We redefine busyness as blessing . . . when in reality it becomes a burden.

Our Creator knows the chaos that we create. Returning to Him refocuses life. Resting in Him results in a replenished life. Surrendering the demands of our schedule to sit at His feet means we find solace, strength and stamina.

Request To Rest. Too often, we define our status by the demands on our schedule. Seemingly, the more we do, the more we are needed. We want to get away, but we can't pry ourselves from the perceived priorities of life. There is no better way to "get away" than to get with God. He longs for us to escape the trials and turmoil of our days by embracing Him. Jesus understands our rigors of responsibility and He responds with a request, *"Come to me, all you who are weary and burdened, and I will give you rest."* (Matt 11:28 NET). We come to Him and He gives rest.

Reason To Rest. The pressures of each day should push us to God's presence, not away. The psalmist cries out, *"And I say, 'Oh, that I had wings like a dove! I would fly away and be at rest.'"* (Ps 55:6 ESV) God designs us to "recycle", not run all the time. Our batteries need to recharge. After Jesus and His disciples met the needs of many, He knew it was time to retreat. Mark writes, *"Then, because so many people were coming and going that they did not even have a chance to eat, He said to them, 'Come with me by yourselves to a quiet place and get some rest.'"* (Mark 6:31 NIV). Spurgeon reminds us, "Rest time is not waste time. It is economy to gather fresh strength . . . It is wisdom to take occasional furlough. In the long run, we shall do more by sometimes doing less."[77]

Results Of Rest. The prophet Jeremiah is crystal clear in his commentary . . . God fully satisfies and fully refreshes. Isaiah tells us *"the Lord gives you rest from your pain, torment, and the hard labor you were forced to do."* (Is 14:3 HCSB) When we reside in our Redeemer's rest, we realize completely renewal, restoration and replenishment. Jesus says, *"Take my yoke on you and learn from me, because I am gentle and humble in heart, and you will find rest for your souls."* (Matt 11:29 NET)

S.D. Gordon writes, "If there be anything that can render the soul calm, dissipate its scruples and dispel its fears, sweeten its sufferings by the anointing of love, impart strength to all its actions, and spread abroad the joy of the Holy Spirit in its countenance and words, it is this simple and childlike repose in the arms of God."[78]

It's okay to step away from the pressure and sit in His presence.

Your God is waiting with outstretched arms, willing to give you a respite and wanting you to find rest . . . run to Him, let Him rescue you and be renewed in His embrace.

KINGDOM THOUGHT 44: FINALLY, HOME

But thank God! He gives us victory over sin and death through our Lord Jesus Christ.
1 Corinthians 15:57 NLT

Recently, we celebrated the home going of a precious lady who lived her life serving our community. We remembered a friend's father who valiantly fought yet surrendered to cancer. A precious young mom who lost her life in a tragic accident. And, a centenarian who served our country, suffered as a POW and contributed a lifetime to his community.

It's never easy losing loved ones. All of us have been touched by loss. A hollowness begins to fill the places within our hearts once filled with everyday hope. Yet, we have an eternal hope found in Heaven . . . God's place of perpetual promise, peace and provision for His people.

Jesus tells us, *"Don't let your hearts be troubled. Trust in God, and trust also in me. There is more than enough room in my Father's home. If this were not so, would I have told you that I am going to prepare a place for you? When everything is ready, I will come and get you, so that you will always be with me where I am."* (John 14:1-3 NLT)

The sting of separation and suffering will be replaced with the hope of Heaven. Our hearts no longer be troubled will triumphantly trust in Him.

No More Sting. The writers of the New Testament describe death having victory and sin having a sting. Those who have experienced the loss of loved ones understand this analogy. Our hearts and our hopes are lanced with the loss. The pain is a prick to our precious memories. Paul tells the Christ-followers in Corinth that the stinger has been removed. He writes, *"But let me reveal to you a wonderful secret. We will not all die, but we will all be transformed! For our dying bodies must be transformed into bodies that will never die; our mortal bodies must be transformed into immortal bodies."* (1 Cor 15:51, 53 NLT). Death is not the end . . . but, an entrance into eternity. Death is no longer victorious . . . it is vanquished. Paul continues, *"For sin is the sting that results in death, and the law gives sin its power. But thank God! He gives us victory over sin and death through our Lord Jesus Christ."* (1 Cor 15:56-57 NLT).

No More Separation. Because of our Savior's love, our loss is never looming. Spurgeon writes, *"When the time comes for you to die, you need not be afraid, because death cannot separate you from God's love."*[79] God's love is not only a passion, but a promise. His promise of his never-ending peace and presence prevails over any power of the enemy. God's love secures us to our Savior. The apostle Paul encourages us, *"For I am sure that neither death nor life, nor angels nor rulers, nor things present nor things to come, nor powers, nor height nor depth, nor anything else in all creation, will be able to separate us from the love of God in Christ Jesus our Lord."* (Rom 8:38-39 ESV).

No More Suffering. God's decisive victory over sin and death gives us deliverance from our suffering. We rest in the assurance of God's abolishing all tears, sorrow, pain and suffering. John records the words of Heaven, *"He will wipe away every tear from their eyes, and death shall be no more, neither shall there be mourning, nor crying, nor pain anymore, for the former things have passed away."* (Rev 21:4 ESV). Everything will be made new.

Jim Hill writes the following hymn of hope:

> *"There is coming a day, when no heartache shall come*
> *No more clouds in the sky,*
> *No more tears to dim our eyes,*
> *All is peace forever more,*
> *On that happy golden shore,*
> *What a day, glorious day that will be."*
> *"They'll be no more sorrow there,*
> *No more burdens to bear,*
> *No more sickness, no more pain,*
> *No more parting over there,*
> *And forever I will be,*
> *With the one who died for me,*
> *What a day, glorious day that will be."*
> *"What a day that will be,*
> *When my Jesus I shall see,*
> *When I look upon His face,*
> *The one who saved me by His grace,*
> *When He takes me by the hand,*
> *And leads me through the promise land,*
> *What a day, Glorious Day that will be."*[80]

Sir Thomas Moore writes, "Earth has no sorrow that Heaven cannot heal."[81]

Those who have gone before us, although deeply missed are sharing in the peace, passion and power of the resurrected Savior.

Our sorrow is replaced with joy. All things will be new. We will see you, soon.

KINGDOM THOUGHT 45: IT'S ON THE WAY

How can someone like me, your servant, talk to You, my Lord? My strength is gone, and I can hardly breathe.
Daniel 10:17 NLT

Have you been to the place where crying out to God becomes so hard, so exhausting and so silent that you want to quit? Praying . . . fasting . . . waiting . . . and nothing happens. There comes a point where the questioning begins . . . Does God care? Is He hearing my cries for help? Do I have the strength to carry on?

The prophet, Daniel knew this kind of anxiety. After receiving insight and instruction from God, the sense and security of God's presence suddenly stopped. For three weeks, Daniel seeks God, but can't find Him.

Finally, a heavenly messenger comes to him and says, *"Don't be afraid, Daniel. Since the first day you began to pray for understanding and to humble yourself before your God, your request has been heard in heaven. I have come in answer to your prayer."* (Dan 10:12 NLT). The delay in God's response was not an indifferent apathy from The Father, but an intentional attack from the foe. The celestial being continues, *"But for twenty-one days the spirit prince of the kingdom of Persia blocked my way. Then Michael, one of the archangels, came to help me, and I left him there with the spirit prince of the kingdom of Persia."* (Daniel 10:13 NLT)

Weak, weary and worn out, Daniel needed encouragement. *"Then the one who looked like a man touched me again, and I felt my strength returning. 'Don't be afraid,' he said, 'for you are very precious to God. Peace! Be encouraged! Be strong!' As he spoke these words to me, I suddenly felt stronger and said to him, 'Please speak to me, my lord, for you have strengthened me.'"* (Dan 10:18-19 NLT)

We Are Precious To God. The messenger's words to Daniel declare God's love for us. Peter reminds us, *"But you are a chosen race, a royal priesthood, a holy nation, a people for His own possession, that you may proclaim the excellencies of Him who called you out of darkness into His marvelous light."* (1 Peter 2:9 ESV). He loves us. He cares for us. We are precious to Him and He is passionate about us.

We Have Peace With God. Because of God's grace, we have His peace. Paul writes, *"Therefore, since we have been justified by faith, we have peace with God through our Lord Jesus Christ. Through Him we have also obtained access by faith into this grace in which we stand, and we rejoice in hope of the glory of God."*

(Rom 5:1-2 ESV). We have peace with God and peace from God. Our persistent prayer opens the door to His promised peace. Paul encourages us, *"Then you will experience God's peace, which exceeds anything we can understand. His peace will guard your hearts and minds as you live in Christ Jesus."* (Phil 4:7 NLT)

We Have Power In God. Daniel writes, *"As he spoke these words to me, I suddenly felt stronger and said to him, 'Please speak to me, my lord, for you have strengthened me.'"* The psalmist tells us, *"He acted with a strong hand and powerful arm. His faithful love endures forever."* (Ps 136:12 NLT). The apostle reminds us, *"For I can do everything through Christ, who gives me strength."* (Phil 4:13 NLT). It's God's power in me, through me and to me. John Piper writes, "It's about the greatness of God, not the significance of man."

German reformer Philip Melanchthen says, "Trouble and perplexity drive me to prayer and prayer drives away perplexity and trouble."[82]

You really need to hear this today . . . I really need to say this today . . .

God will NEVER LEAVE . . .

God will ALWAYS LOVE . . .

God will ALWAYS LEAD!

Have confidence in Him . . . cling to him . . . cry out to Him. The answer is on the way.

Kingdom Thought 46: Trusting

Trust in the Lord with all your heart; do not depend on your own understanding. Seek His will in all you do, and He will show you which path to take.
Proverbs 3:5-6 NLT

Line them all up and I've made more mistakes than had milestones.

We all mess up. It may be out of ignorance, incompetence, inattention, indifference, inability or even intentionally . . . for whatever the reason . . . we all make mistakes.

All mistakes have consequences. We hope that we receive grace and mercy from community. Yet, we have the ability and availability to rest in the Grace-giver and Mercy-mover. Solomon gives us a simple and proactive formula for our stupidity and errors in judgement.

Our Conviction. Too many times we trust more in our own insightful whims, than in God's inspirational wisdom. We need to trust ALL in Him with ALL our heart. It is complete conviction. The psalmist writes, *"Commit everything you do to the Lord. Trust Him, and He will help you."* (Ps 37:5 NLT). Depending primarily on our own insights only leads to perpetuating instability. The book of Proverbs reminds us, *"Whoever trusts in his own mind is a fool, but he who walks in wisdom will be delivered."* (Prov 28:26 ESV)

Our Consent. Another translation reads, *"in all your ways, acknowledge Him . . ."*. It's recognizing that we have limited reasoning, response or resource on our own . . . He has and is all that we need. Our approach can often lead to anxiety, apathy or abandonment. In our Prince of Peace, there is no anxiety. With our Wonderful Counselor, there is no apathy. With our Everlasting Father, there is no abandonment. Prayer becomes our confession of conceding to our Creator. Paul writes, *"do not be anxious about anything, but in everything by prayer and supplication with thanksgiving let your requests be made known to God."* (Phil 4:6 ESV)

Our Confidence. Resting and relying on God's complete and absolute guidance grounds us in His amazing grace. Paul reminds us, *"And we know that God causes everything to work together for the good of those who love God and are called according to His purpose for them."* (Rom 8:28 NLT). It's not a "think so" . . . or "hope so" . . . it's a "know so". There is no doubt in God's decisive directing. Solomon tells us that *"He will show you which path to take".* God's direction becomes our delight and our deliverance.

Bottom line . . . we are all going to make some bad choices, stupid mistakes or have errors in judgement. Famed UCLA basketball coach and mentor of young men, John Wooden reminds us, "If you're not making mistakes, then you're not doing anything. I'm positive that a doer makes mistakes."[83]

Even in those dark and uncertain times, we have the conviction that He can be trusted, we consent to follow His direction, and we have confidence that He will guide.

Trust and seek . . . God will direct and deliver.

So, to all of us who mess-up every day . . . we have a Help and we have a Hope.

KINGDOM THOUGHT 47: IT'S A TRAP

Fearing people is a dangerous trap, trusting The Lord means safety.
Proverbs 29:25 NLT

Augustine writes, "Fear is the response of the human heart when it's one thing is threatened."[84]

Solomon is credited with being one of the wisest and wealthiest who ever lived. Yet, the threats to his treasured things created terror. He fought his own fears . . . fear of failure, fear of people, fear of loss, fear of loneliness. With insight, Solomon provides a "solutionary" strategy for the snares that surround us.

We Have Protection In Our Fears. Fear is a subtle snare of our enemy. It traps us with terror that will tear the very fiber of our faith. Solomon finds security and safety in his Sovereign. The psalmist reminds us that trust is the key, *"But when I am afraid, I will put my trust in You."* (Psalms 56:3 NLT) A. B. Simpson writes, "Fear is born of Satan, and if we would only take time to think a moment we would see that everything Satan says is founded upon a falsehood. Every fear is distrust, and trust is the remedy for fear."

We Have Peace In Our Fears. God calls us to calm. Proverbs reminds us, *"But all who listen to Me will live in peace, untroubled by fear of harm."* (Prov 1:33 NLT) Spurgeon teaches, "Whether the fear arise from without or within, from past, present, or future, from temporals, or spirituals, from men or devils, let us maintain faith, and we shall soon recover courage."[85] God commits His calm and courage in the confusion of our chaos. Jesus tells us, *"I am leaving you with a gift—peace of mind and heart. And the peace I give is a gift the world cannot give. So don't be troubled or afraid."* (John 14:27 NLT)

We Have Promise In Our Fears. Paul reminds us, *"For God has not given us a spirit of fear and timidity, but of power, love, and self-discipline."* (2 Tim 1:7 NLT). Fear cannot thrive where faith is alive. To survive in our fears, we must surrender to faith. God's word is true, tested and tried . . . He has not given us fear, but favor. John encourages us, *"Such love has no fear, because perfect love expels all fear. If we are afraid, it is for fear of punishment, and this shows that we have not fully experienced his perfect love."* (1 John 4:18 NLT) We rest in His promise, in His passion and in His rock-solid, always powerful hands that never let go.

We share the same struggles as Solomon. Learning for his experiences allows us to live in his example. John Bunyan reminds us of our remedy, "Let it rain, let it blow, let it thunder, let it lightning, a Christian must still believe. 'At what time,' said the good man, 'I am afraid, I will trust in thee.'"[86]

Shirley Caesar writes the following encouraging lyrics;

> *"When the world that I've been*
> *Living in collapses at my feet.*
> *And when my life is all tattered and torn.*
> *Though I'm wind-swept, I've been battered*
> *I'm gonna cling unto His cross.*
> *I'll find peace in the midst of the storm."*
> *There is peace in the midst of the storm-tossed life.*
> *There is an Anchor, there is a rock to build my faith upon.*
> *Jesus Christ is my vessel, so I fear no alarm.*
> *He gives me peace in the midst of the storm."*[87]

Fight your fears with faith and turn your terrors with trust.

He is the Peace in the midst of your storm.

KINGDOM THOUGHT 48: EYES ON HIM

Don't be afraid, for I am with you. Don't be discouraged, for I am your God. I will strengthen you and help you. I will hold you up with My victorious right hand.
Isaiah 41:10 NLT

I can't tell you how many times I feel like quitting.

Sometimes it's every day . . . and, sometimes its several times during the day.

Candidly, the pressure can be too much.

The problems become too many.

And, the pain can be too unbearable.

Many of us have learned to "go for it", "gut it out" and "give it our all". Sometimes it's just not enough. We're encouraged to be decisive, deliberate and determined . . . but determination can often be diminished by despair, disillusionment or defeat.

In our fear . . . failure . . . and fatigue, we are reminded by the prophet Isaiah that God was with the nation of Israel and He is always with us, He gives us strength and He will help. Here are some more promises about our ever-present and all-powerful God.

He Is Our Source. *"The LORD is my strength and shield. I trust him with all my heart. He helps me, and my heart is filled with joy. I burst out in songs of thanksgiving."* (Ps 28:7 NLT). He is the One I can trust, and He is worthy of my trust. He gives grace and I respond with gratitude. There is no other source or supply that will satisfy.

He Is Our Strength. Paul tells us of his personal strength, *"I can do all things through Christ who strengthens me."* (Phil 4:13 NLT) To the followers in Ephesus, he writes, *"Finally, be strong in the Lord and in the strength of His might."* (Eph.6:10 ESV) The psalmist identifies God's protecting and perfecting power, *"It is God who arms me with strength and keeps my way secure."* (Ps 18:32 NIV). When I am collapsing in weakness, He is completing His work.

He Is Our Security. Jehovah God says, *"Have I not commanded you? Be strong and courageous. Do not be afraid; do not be discouraged, for the Lord your God will be with you wherever you go."* (Josh 1:9 NIV) God's surrounding security makes me safe. Moses tells us that God will never abort His care or abandon His presence, *"Be strong and courageous. Do not be afraid or terrified because of them, for the Lord your God goes with you; He will never leave you nor forsake you."* (Deut 31:6 NIV). He will always care, and He will always be there.

He Is Our Stability. The psalmist writes, *"He alone is my rock and my salvation, my fortress where I will never be shaken."* (Ps 62:2 NLT). When our walk seems shaky and uncertain, Jesus is there to secure our insecurity and stabilize our instability. Pope Francis reminds us, "We cannot live as Christians separate from the rock who is Christ. He gives us strength and stability, but also joy and serenity."[88] When the calamity of life's storms hit, He is the calm.

Feel like quitting? Me, too. I'm reminded of the encouragement from the writer of Hebrews, *"We do this by keeping our eyes on Jesus, the champion who initiates and perfects our faith. Because of the joy awaiting him, He endured the cross, disregarding its shame. Now He is seated in the place of honor beside God's throne."* (Heb 12:2 NLT)

God is our source. He is our strength. He gives us security. And, He alone is our life's stability.

Let's keep our eyes on Him . . . focused by faith and faithfully following.

KINGDOM THOUGHT 49: YES, I CAN

I have strength for all things in Christ Who empowers me [I am ready for anything and equal to anything through Him Who infuses inner strength into me; I am self-sufficient in Christ's sufficiency.]
Philippians 4:13 AMP

There's an inner power that develops when we understand that we're not strong enough. At the intersection of fear and adversity is the crosswalk of a confident strength more powerful than our own. Living life is about confronting fears, finding inner strength and doing what's right in the face of adversity.

The apostle Paul reminds Christ-followers that his ability to persevere with persistence and power is only found in the Savior who gives him strength. How can we plug into His power?

Recognize Our Weaknesses. It's good to identify our insecurities and recognize our weaknesses. This introspection keeps us longing for and looking to God. Paul writes to struggling believers in Corinth, *"Each time He said, 'My grace is all you need. My power works best in weakness.' So now I am glad to boast about my weaknesses, so that the power of Christ can work through me. That's why I take pleasure in my weaknesses, and in the insults, hardships, persecutions, and troubles that I suffer for Christ. For when I am weak, then I am strong."* (2 Cor 12:9-10 NLT). We embrace and express our weaknesses . . . and then we experience His grace.

Realize His Working. An advisor, Hanani told King Asa of Judah, *"For the eyes of the Lord run to and fro throughout the whole earth, to give strong support to those whose heart is blameless toward him."* (2 Chron 16:9 ESV). It's not uncommon for us to try to fit our days into a predetermined and preconceived format, controlled by our schedules and systems. The eyes of God are watching our present and our future, understanding what we need before the need arises. Take a moment . . . relax in His control . . . and, see how He is working. The prophet Isaiah, reminds us of God's promise, *"Fear not, for I am with you; be not dismayed, for I am your God; I will strengthen you, I will help you, I will uphold you with my righteous right hand."* (Is 41:10 ESV)

Rest In His Worship. Paul tells young Timothy, *"For God has not given us a spirit of fear and timidity, but of power, love, and self-discipline."* (2 Tim 1:7 NLT) Young gives inspiration with a thought from God, *"When you look to Me and whisper My Name, you break free and receive My help. Focus on Me, and you will find Peace in My Presence."*[89] The prophet Zephaniah encourages the weak nation of Israel, *"For the Lord your God is living among you. He is a mighty Savior."* (Zeph 3:17 NLT) In our weariness from struggle and weakness in strength . . . we worship and find serenity and safety.

D.L. Moody, in the margins of his Bible between the fifth and sixth chapters of the Gospel of John, between Jesus' claim to be the Son of God and the miraculous feeding of over five thousand, he wrote, "If God by your partner, make your plans large."[90] Be encouraged today and make God your partner.

When we surrender to God's strength, we recognize our weakness, realize He is working, and we rest in His worship.

KINGDOM THOUGHT 50: TOUGH GET GOING

That is why we never give up. Though our bodies are dying, our spirits are being renewed every day. For our present troubles are small and won't last very long. Yet they produce for us a glory that vastly outweighs them and will last forever! So, we don't look at the troubles we can see now; rather, we fix our gaze on things that cannot be seen. For the things we see now will soon be gone, but the things we cannot see will last forever.
2 Corinthians 4:16-18 NLT

In every challenge, we are provided with a choice . . . believe in the process or be burdened with the problem.

There's an old adage attributed to famed Notre Dame football coach Knute Rockne, "When the going gets tough, the tough get going."[91]

The daily grind often produces a debilitating grief. But those who endure will engage . . . the promise of everlasting hope gives us everyday help.

The apostle writes, *". . . And as God's grace reaches more and more people, there will be great thanksgiving, and God will receive more and more glory."* (2 Cor 4:15 NLT) Paul provides road signs to guide us on this potential and promising journey.

Our Resolve. *"That is why we never give up."* Paul's conviction is to never concede. Often, our defeat is birthed in our denial that the Divine will deliver us. Don't give up. Franklin D. Roosevelt says, "When you come to the end of your rope, tie a knot and hang on."[92] The apostle reminds us, *"But as for you, be strong and do not give up, for your work will be rewarded."* (2 Chron 15:7 NIV) Perseverance with purpose from above is powerful.

Our Renewal. Renewal and refreshment lead to our replenishment. These bodies wear down and wear out, yet our minds are made new and our spirits are sustained. Isaiah tells us, *"But those who hope in the Lord will renew their strength. They will soar on wings like eagles; they will run and not grow weary; they will walk and not be faint."* (Is 40:31 NIV)

Our Reason. In the time frame of eternity, our trials are tiny and temporary. Paul reminds us, *"For our momentary, light suffering is producing for us an eternal weight of glory far beyond all comparison."* (2 Cor 4:17 NET). Any grief is our gain with a result of God's grace and growing glory. Peter encourages us, *"And, after you have suffered for a little while, the God of all grace who called you to his eternal glory in Christ will himself restore, confirm, strengthen, and establish you."* (1 Pet 5:10 NET)

Our Recognition. Perspective is the ability to peer into God's plan and trust in God's purpose. Paul describes it as recognizing the eternal triumph over the everyday trial. Our seeing impacts our being. Churchill said, "The pessimist sees difficulty in every opportunity. The optimist sees opportunity in every difficulty."[93] An eternal optimist sees all opportunities and obstacles from God's observatory . . . hope and promise from a heavenly perspective.

When you feel like giving up, get up.

When you feel like groaning, be grateful.

When you can't see with your eyes, see with His.

Allow God's determination to drive you, deliver you and define you for your good and His glory.

KINGDOM THOUGHT 51: DESTINY OR DISASTER

Now when they saw the boldness of Peter and John, and perceived that they were uneducated, common men, they were astonished. And they recognized that they had been with Jesus.
Acts 4:13 ESV

Peter and John were both fisherman by trade and they came from a small city that had little economic or cultural significance.

Paul, although theologically trained, was a tent maker.

Matthew was a tax collector.

Onesimus was a runaway slave.

Cornelius was a soldier.

Rahab was a prostitute.

Moses was a murderer.

David was a conspiring adulterer.

The list goes on and on. Yet, all of these experienced a sense of Kingdom greatness because of grace.

Peter and John tell others what they have seen, heard and experienced . . . they are confident, not condemning. They are not only identified as being with Jesus . . . they are impacted, influenced and inspired by Jesus.

This brand of authenticity, boldness and courage becomes the new "ABC's" of following God. It isn't their education . . . it's their experience with Jesus. It isn't a position; it is His presence. It isn't sitting at the feet of an educator; it's sitting at the feet of The Master Teacher.

These "uneducated, common men" astonish the traditionalists of the day because they accept the truth of Jesus.

Jesus Changes. Paul writes to the Christ-followers in Corinth, *"This means that anyone who belongs to Christ has become a new person. The old life is gone; a new life has begun!"* (2 Cor 5:17 NLT) We are no longer in chains, we change. We are free from our past and penalties of sin. We are given a promise and peace through our pain and problems. Jesus says, *"So if the Son sets you free, you are truly free."* (John 8:36 NLT)

Jesus Challenges. A life changed by Jesus challenges the culture . . . with compassion, not condemnation. It's triumph, not timidity. It's hope, not hopelessness. We are light to the darkness and salt to the tasteless. Jesus says, *"No one lights a lamp and then puts it under a basket. Instead, a lamp is placed* *on a stand, where it gives light to everyone in the house. In the same way, let your good deeds shine out for all to see, so that everyone will praise your heavenly Father."* (Matt 5:15-16 NLT). Light illuminates the way. Salt infuses flavor so others can *"taste and see that The Lord is good".* (Ps 34:8)

Instead of a fisherman, tent maker, or tax collector, you may be an executive, small business owner, salesman, educator, barista, stay-at-home mom, coach, virtual employee or service provider.

We all experience Kingdom greatness and grace . . . not because of prominence, position, power or paycheck . . . but, because we have been in the presence of our Creator.

God defines each of us as a destiny maker . . . by changing us and challenging us.

This is a day of tender boldness, of truthful bravery and of letting others know that you have truly been with Jesus.

KINGDOM THOUGHT 52: HE IS ABLE

Therefore, He is able, once and forever, to save those who come to God through Him. He lives forever to intercede with God on their behalf.
Hebrews 7:25 NLT

Ability is never the same as availability. Many people have the talent . . . but, few have the time. Jesus is one who always can complete any task needed within His will . . . He always does. He is true. He is faithful. He is Almighty, all-caring, all-knowing and ever-present.

In 1958, Paul E. Paino wrote these lyrics to a loved chorus . . .

> *"He's able, He's able, I know He's able; I know my Lord is able to carry me through.*
> *He healed the broken-hearted and set the captive free;*
> *He made the lame to walk again and caused the blind to see.*
> *He's able, He's able, I know He's able; I know my Lord is able to carry me through."*[94]

He Is Always Able. The writer of a letter to Hebrew believers writes, *"He (Jesus) is able, once and forever . . . "*. He has all ability and capability. Our Lord lacks nothing. Our Savior is more than sufficient. Our Redeemer is ready. He saves those who come to God, through Him . . . in times past and in times forward. Paul writes to his young follower Timothy of God's securing safety, *"That is why I am suffering here in prison. But I am not ashamed of it, for I know the One in whom I trust, and I am sure that He is able to guard what I have entrusted to him until the day of His return."* (2 Tim 1:12 NLT) Paul also writes about Abraham's faith as he trusted God's ability in promise keeping, *"Abraham never wavered in believing God's promise. In fact, his faith grew stronger, and in this he brought glory to God. He was fully convinced that God is able to do whatever he promises."* (Rom 4:20-21 NLT) And, to the believers in Ephesus, the apostle validates the power of God, *"Now all glory to God, who is able, through His mighty power at work within us, to accomplish infinitely more than we might ask or think."* (Eph 3:20 NLT)

He Is Always Interceding. The writer of Hebrews tells us that Jesus *"lives forever to intercede with God"* on our behalf. Take a moment to let that sink in. Jesus is alive and He will live forever. And, He . . . The Son Of God . . . The Resurrected Christ . . . The Anointed One . . . The Victorious One . . . The King of all Kings . . . Jesus is interceding with God on your behalf. This may be too detailed . . . but, He is interceding "with" God, not "to" God. Jesus, the Son and God, the Father are jointly working on your behalf . . . praying, planning, protecting, purposing . . . all for you and all for me. Jesus' prayer is recorded by John, *"I am praying not only for these disciples but also for all who will ever believe in Me through their message. I pray that they will all be one, just as You and I are one—as You are in me, Father, and I am in you. And may they be in Us so that the world will believe you sent Me."* (John 17:20-21 NLT)

An edition of an 1825 newspaper solicited military aids and volunteers who were "willing and ready and able". We enter confidently into His throne room of grace in our time of need and find Jesus ready, willing and able to help. The author of Hebrews reminds us, *"So let us come boldly to the throne of our gracious God. There we will receive His mercy, and we will find grace to help us when we need it most."* (Heb 4:16 NLT)

Today . . . know that your God is able to carry you through.

KINGDOM THOUGHT 53: ALL THINGS

And we know that God causes everything to work together for the good of those who love God and are called according to His purpose for them.
Romans 8:28 NLT

I often wonder if things are going to work out or how things are going to work out . . . and during all that time . . . God is seemingly working them out.

The apostle Paul gives the believers in Rome a glimpse into God's "behind the scenes" grace and guidance.

His Assistance. Before telling of God's control, Paul reminds us of His comforting counsel and communication. Through His Spirit, God is working in our weaknesses. Paul writes, *"And the Holy Spirit helps us in our weakness. For example, we don't know what God wants us to pray for. But the Holy Spirit prays for us with groanings that cannot be expressed in words. And the Father who knows all hearts knows what the Spirit is saying, for the Spirit pleads for us believers in harmony with God's own will."* (Rom 8:26-27 NLT). The Holy Spirit prays in perfect partnership for us while promoting God's own will.

Our Assurance. Paul reassures the Christ followers in Rome with three confirming words . . . *"And we know"*. The word chosen in the original language means "an experiential knowledge". It's not just in our head as a fact, it's in our heart as a familiarity. James uses the same word in his encouraging comments regarding trials and difficulties, *"Consider it a sheer gift, friends, when tests and challenges come at you from all sides. You know that under pressure, your faith-life is forced into the open and shows its true colors. So don't try to get out of anything prematurely. Let it do its work, so you become mature and well-developed, not deficient in any way."* (Jam 1:2-4 MSG)

His Action. I don't understand how. I can't explain it. It's beyond me. It's difficult because we live our lives with a "cause and effect" way of thinking. Our God is not concerned with the effect, because He is the cause. Paul tells *us "that God causes everything to work together for the good of those who love"* Him and these are *"called according to His purpose for them."* He is the Sovereign Multi-Tasker. He has been involved in our yesterday as He impacts our today and influences our tomorrow. Scotty Smith writes, "Nothing in our past has marked us as a 'Plan B' people; nothing in our present contradicts the promise of Your care or the pledge of Your presence; nothing in our future will separate us from the wonders of Your love or alter the completion of Your plan."[95] He sees and understands it all . . . our past, present and future.

Our Acceptance. God's grace not only guides, but it grants us acceptance with Him. He loves and accepts based on His passion and promises, not on our performance . . . *"And having called them, He gave them right standing with Himself. And having given them right standing, He gave them His glory."* (Romans 8:30 NLT). John Gill describes God's absolute acceptance, "not by effort, but by special grace; from darkness to light, from bondage to liberty, from the company of sinful men to fellowship with Christ, from a trust in their own righteousness to a dependence on His, to grace here, and glory hereafter; which is done according to the purpose of God".

Smith shares portions of his practical and powerful prayer from Romans 8:28 . . .

> *"You are a God at work."*
>
> *"You are presently working in all things for Your glory and for our good."*
>
> *"You work in all things for our good, not merely for our liking."*
>
> *"Our foolish hearts often call good things evil and evil things good. Our demanding hearts often treat You like Sugar Daddy, rather than Abba, Father."*
>
> *"Our impatient hearts would settle for the fool's gold of immediate relief, rather than wait for the lasting treasure of eternal inheritance."*
>
> *"Thank You for not giving into our whining and spirit of entitlement."*
>
> *"We praise You for not giving us everything we want, because we often ask for things that will simply make life easier, rather than trust You for things that will make us like Jesus."*[96]

You may not see it . . . but, believe it. God is working.

KINGDOM THOUGHT 54: PRACTICE AND PERFECT

Keep putting into practice all you learned and received from me— everything you heard from me and saw me doing. Then the God of peace will be with you.
Philippians 4:9 NLT

How many times have we heard, "In one ear and out the other"? Selective listening in response to God's word can lead to fear overcoming our faith.

The truth we hear and see can sometimes be replaced by what we calculate and try to figure out. We can embrace the idea of a peace that protects our thoughts and feelings, yet we often ignore the prescriptive remedy of following truth. God guarantees a *"peace that surpasses all understanding"*. (Phil 4:7)

Paul affirms the benefit of being a "doer" not just a "hearer" of the God's truth. James writes, *"But don't just listen to God's word. You must do what it says. Otherwise, you are only fooling yourselves."* (James 1:22 NLT)

Practiced Precepts. Our peace, pleasure and prosperity come from putting His principles into practice. The psalmist reminds us, *"Oh, the joys of those who do not follow the advice of the wicked, or stand around with sinners, or join in with mockers. But they delight in the law of the Lord, meditating on it day and night. They are like trees planted along the riverbank, bearing fruit each season. Their leaves never wither, and they prosper in all they do."* (Ps 1:1-3 NLT). God's truths are not only remembered in our head but reside in our hearts. We recall them, recite them, rehearse them and relive them. His word becomes our meditation and our message while giving our life meaning.

Powered Prayer. When fear overshadows our faith, worry overrides our worship. Paul writes, *"Don't worry about anything; instead, pray about everything. Tell God what you need and thank Him for all He has done."* (Phil 4:6 NLT). Giving our anxieties over to God, with appreciation and gratitude allows God to apply His grace. Our prayer becomes purposeful, praise-filled and powerful. Note that we *"thank Him for all He has done"*, not for what He will do. Powered prayer is not longing in the tomorrows of what could be but living in the today of what God is doing. He is working . . . here and now.

Promised Peace. Safety in God is simplified when we seek His truth. Paul confirms God's promise, *"Then (when we practice truth) the God of peace will be with you."* (Phil 4:9 AMP) C. S. Lewis writes, "God cannot give us a happiness and peace apart from Himself, because it is not there. There is no such thing."[97] In his letter to the Christ followers in Corinth, the apostle illustrates the evidences of living God's truth in our everyday, "Be joyful. Grow to maturity. Encourage each other. Live in harmony and peace. Then the God of love and peace will be with you." (2 Cor 13:11 NLT)

Joy . . .

Maturity . . .

Encouragement . . .

Harmony . . .

Peace . . . these are the fruits of following truth. God always keeps His word by His Word.

His peace is promised to those who put His promises into practice.

When we live in the truth, we live in triumph.

KINGDOM THOUGHTS 55: YOU CAN TRUST HIM

My blessing is on those people who trust in Me, who put their confidence in Me.
Jeremiah 17:7 NET

Trust is belief in honesty and reliability. It's complete confidence in a person, promise, purpose or plan. Trust has been described as a dependable, an unshakable and a sustainable relationship.

Unless it's based on wholehearted faith, trust can be fragile and easily broken.

For those who have been wounded, hurt or abused; trust is not an immediate response. Our own fears and failures can taint our trust. Solomon encourages us, *"Trust in the Lord with all your heart, and do not lean on your own understanding."* (Prov 3:5 ESV). Author Stephen Covey identifies trust as being based on a proven person or process. He writes, "Once you create trust—genuine character and competence-based trust—almost everything else falls into place."[98] Solomon continues his thought, "In all your ways acknowledge Him, and He will make straight your paths." (Prov 3:6 ESV)

Trust In His Character. David gives us an assurance, "Those who know Your name trust in You, for You, O Lord, do not abandon those who search for You." (Ps 9:10 NLT) God's name and character . . . the essence of Who He is and the excellence in what He does . . . gives us confidence and conviction. What He says He will do. Solomon shares a wise insight, *"Every word of God is pure; He is a shield to those who put their trust in Him."* (Prov 30:5 NKJV)

Trust In His Competency. Too often we enter into a battle of wills with God. Our understanding is limited . . . His is limitless. Our power is weak, but His strength is all-powerful. We make our ways crooked and He makes them straight. Our God can handle any and all of our chaos, conflicts and confusion. The psalmist writes, *"The Lord is my rock and my fortress and my deliverer; My God, my strength, in whom I will trust; My shield and the horn of my salvation, my stronghold."* (Ps 18:2 NKJV). God's got skills. I can trust Him.

Trust In His Compassion. King David writes of his trust in God's unfailing, unending and unwavering love, *"For the king trusts in the Lord. The unfailing love of the Most High will keep him from stumbling."* (Ps 21:7 NLT). When we thrive in His presence, we trust in His passion. The psalmist writes, *"But I am like an olive tree, thriving in the house of God. I will always trust in God's unfailing love."* (Ps 52:8 NLT). He loves us and He will never stop loving us. It's not about what we do . . . it's about what He did. Paul reminds us, *"But God showed his great love* *for us by sending Christ to die for us while we were still sinners."* (Rom 5:8 NLT)

Trust In His Care. Peter tells us, *"Give all your worries and cares to God, for He cares about you."* (1 Pet 5:7 NLT). Even when we can't see how God is leading, we can surround ourselves with His loving care. The psalmist encourages us, "Give your burdens to the Lord, and He will take care of you. He will not permit the godly to slip and fall." (Ps 55:22 NLT).

A little girl and her father were crossing a bridge.

The father was concerned for his daughter so he asked, "Sweetheart, would you please hold my hand so that you don't fall into the river?"

The little girl said: "No, Daddy. You hold my hand."

"What's the difference?" Asked the puzzled father.

"There's a big difference," replied the little girl.

"If I hold your hand and something happens to me, chances are that I may let your hand go. But if you hold my hand, I know for sure that no matter what happens, you will never let my hand go."[99]

In your storms, struggles or surprises, hold on to His hand . . . trust His character, trust His competency, trust His compassion and trust His care . . . He will never let go of you.

KINGDOM THOUGHT 56: MAKING PEACE

These things I have spoken to you, that in Me you may have peace. In the world you will have tribulation; but be of good cheer, I have overcome the world.
John 16:33 NKJV

Nearing the end of His life, Jesus begins preparing His followers for the life changing challenges they will soon face. In the midst of describing His death and their persecution, He reassures them of His peace that will soon be their peace.

In each of our journeys, we face times of chaos, confusion and conflicts. The storms of life produce struggles that can often lead to shipwreck. Opposition and obstacles can be overwhelming.

With certain confidence, Jesus knows that peace is found in His promises, in His power and in His presence. The prophet Isaiah reminds us, *"For a child is born to us, a Son is given to us. The government will rest on His shoulders. And He will be called: Wonderful Counselor, Mighty God, Everlasting Father, Prince of Peace. His government and its peace will never end . . ."* (Is 9:6-7 NLT)

Peace With God. Paul reminds us, *"Since we have been made right in God's sight by faith, we have peace with God because of what Jesus Christ our Lord has done for us."* (Rom 5:1 NLT) Separation from God because of sin is no more. Christ paid the price of our redemption and reconciled our relationship with the Creator. Eugene Peterson, in his paraphrase, The Message writes, *"Christ brought us together through His death on the cross. The Cross brought us to embrace and that was the end of the hostility. Christ came and preached peace to outsiders and provided peace as insiders. He treated us as equals and thus made us equals. Through Him we both share the same Spirit and have equal access to the Father."* (Eph 2:16-18 MSG).

Peace With Others. Acceptance from God . . . Acceptance with others. Paul closes his letter to those in Corinth with these encouraging words, *"Be joyful. Grow to maturity. Encourage each other. Live in harmony and peace. Then the God of love and peace will be with you."* (2 Cor 13:11 NLT). Walking in harmony is better than running in hostility . . . wisdom over warring. James reminds us, *"Wisdom from above is first of all pure. It is also peace loving, gentle at all times, and willing to yield to others. It is full of mercy and the fruit of good deeds. It shows no favoritism and is always sincere. And those who are peacemakers will plant seeds of peace and reap a harvest of righteousness."* (Jam 3:17-18 NLT)

Peace With Ourselves. This is the tough one. Often our past conflicts keep us from our own personal calm. We may no longer cause hurt in others, but we can't heal ourselves. We may experience forgiveness from God, express forgiveness to others and yet never enjoy forgiveness in our own hearts. Paul reminds us of a life-changing truth, *"So now there is no condemnation for those who belong to Christ Jesus."* (Rom 8:1 NLT) God no longer sees our sin. It's forgiven and forgotten. We learn from it but we don't live in it.

Oswald Chambers, Principal of the Bible Training College in London, reflects on experiencing peace from God and peace with God, "I have to get to the point of the absolute and unquestionable relationship that takes everything exactly as it comes from Him. God never guides us at some time in the future, but always here and now. Realize that the Lord is here now, and the peace you receive is immediate."[100]

His peace destines us, delights us, and delivers us.

Find Him . . . find His peace.

KINGDOM THOUGHT 57: HANG IN THERE

O my people, trust in Him at all times. Pour out your heart to Him, for God is our refuge. Selah
Psalms 62:8 NLT

It's often easier to commune with God in the calmness of the morning, as opposed to calling out to Him in the chaos of the day. As each day begins with the excitement of new opportunities, it can end with the exhaustion of never-ending oppositions and obstacles.

Our God is there at the start of each day . . . and, He is there in every struggle we may encounter throughout the day. He is the God of the early morning and the God of every moment. He is there in every situation, in each second, with a ready solution.

The psalmist writes, *"Morning, noon, and night I cry out in my distress, and the LORD hears my voice."* (Ps 55:17 NLT)

Challenges are not chastisement.

Problems are not punishment.

Adversity is not admonishment.

Challenges are changed in His control.

Problems are placated in His presence.

Adversity is addressed with His attention.

Trust In Him Because He Is Worthy Of Your Trust. Solomon shares his wisdom with us, *"Trust in the LORD with all your heart; do not depend on your own understanding. Seek His will in all you do, and He will show you which path to take."* (Prov 3:5-6 NLT). Our understanding is limited by our situations . . . His is unlimited because of His sovereignty. When we are tossed and turned, He can be trusted. In our time of help, He wants all of our heart.

Rest In Him Because He Is Your Refuge. In order to find rest, we must reside in Him. The psalmist reminds us, *"Those who live in the shelter of the Most High will find rest in the shadow of the Almighty. This I declare about the LORD: He alone is my refuge, my place of safety; He is my God, and I trust Him."* (Ps 91:1-2 NLT).

Selah recorded the following lyrics:

> *"You are my hiding place.*
> *You always fill my heart with songs of deliverance.*
> *Whenever I am afraid, I will trust in You."*

Call Out To Him Because He Hears Your Cry. The collection of Psalms gives us comfort . . . *"The LORD hears his people when they call to Him for help. He rescues them from all their troubles. The LORD is close to the brokenhearted; He rescues those whose spirits are crushed. The righteous person faces many troubles, but the LORD comes to the rescue each time."* (Ps 34:17-19 NLT). He hears each time and every time. Martin Luther encourages us, "All who call on God in true faith, earnestly from the heart, will certainly be heard, and will receive what they have asked and desired."[101] David reminds us, *"Then call on Me when you are in trouble, and I will rescue you, and you will give Me glory."* (Ps 50:15 NLT). Cry out . . . call to Him . . . and He will comfort.

Instead of resting in the "poor is me", resolve to pour your heart to Him.

In every hour He will be your help.

In every minute He will be your miracle.

In every second He will be your source.

In His time . . . we will be defended . . . we will be delivered . . . we will be (re)defined.

We're on His schedule.

KINGDOM THOUGHT 58: MASTERPIECE

And I am certain that God, who began the good work within you, will continue His work until it is finally finished on the day when Christ Jesus returns.
Philippians 1:6 NLT

Fine craftsmanship is an art that should be deeply appreciated.

A watchmaker will hand assemble, polish and fit over 115 parts to make a fine timepiece. An artist can apply thousands of brushstrokes utilizing multiple hues to create a one-of-a-kind work. A chef can take the simplest ingredients and create a complex culinary delight.

The artistry of a master is evidenced in his masterpiece.

Paul reminds us, *"For we are God's masterpiece. He has created us anew in Christ Jesus, so we can do the good things he planned for us long ago."* (Eph 2:10 NLT)

The apostle displays a certainty and confidence that what God begins, He will always finish.

He Creates. At the moment of surrender, God begins a supernatural work in each of us. Paul writes to the Christ-followers in Ephesus, *"But God is so rich in mercy, and He loved us so much, that even though we were dead because of our sins, He gave us life when He raised Christ from the dead. (It is only by God's grace that you have been saved!)"* (Eph 2:4, 5 NLT). Our hearts are focused on selfishness, but God frees us with salvation. Death to life. Grave to grace. The apostle reminds us. "Therefore, if anyone is in Christ, he is a new creation. The old has passed away; behold, the new has come." (2 Cor 5:17 ESV)

He Continues. We are not left alone in the process of becoming new creations in Christ. We are clay in the Potter's hand. The prophet Jeremiah records God's illustration *"and he reworked [the clay] into another vessel, as it seemed good to the potter to do."* (Jer 18:4 ESV). He softens and He shapes until He is satisfied. Glyer writes, "As God hovers over His creation, centering us or shaping us or even restoring us from collapse, He may transform us in ways we never imagined."[102] The psalmist encourages with God's attentiveness, *"The Lord will fulfill his purpose for me; Your steadfast love, O Lord, endures forever. Do not forsake the work of your hands."* (Ps 138:8 ESV).

He Completes. God finishes what He starts. Henry Spence-Jones writes, "The good work is God's; He began it and He will perfect it."[103] The apostle Paul encourages believers in Corinth with these words, *"I give thanks to my God* *always for you because of the grace of God that was given you in Christ Jesus . . . who will sustain you to the end, guiltless in the day of our Lord Jesus Christ."* (1 Cor 1:4, 8 ESV). In complete confidence, we trust in His finished work . . . free of guilt and full of grace.

Max Lucado encourages us, "God sees us with the eyes of a Father. He sees our defects, errors and blemishes. But He also sees our value."[104]

You are God's masterpiece in the making . . . and the Master Craftsman is good at what He does.

Kingdom Thought 59: Caring and Carrying

I will be your God throughout your lifetime—until your hair is white with age. I made you, and I will care for you. I will carry you along and save you.
Isaiah 46:4 NLT

My wife and I have a number of friends who are walking through confusing and challenging days. They often feel afflicted, abandoned and alone. The looming question, "Will this ever end?" is always in the forefront of their fight.

Often, in our raging storms, while being tossed back and forth, there is little relief. Hope is the only anchor that secures the drifting boat of our burdens.

He Is Committed. Jehovah God reminds Isaiah of the promise of His never-ending presence. God says, *"I will be your God throughout your lifetime"*. In good times and bad . . . through hope and heartache . . . through blessing and brokenness . . . from the beginning to the end . . . God is there. God will not only be present . . . it's also personal. The great "I Am" says that He is all ours. God is not distant, He is deliberate. God not elusive, He is exclusive. God is never absent; He has perfect attendance.

He Is Creator. Isaiah is encouraged with God's words, "I made you". We are made in His image, with a longing to be His child and loving His compassion. Paul reminds us *"For we are God's masterpiece. He has created us anew in Christ Jesus, so we can do the good things He planned for us long ago".* (Eph 2:10 NLT)

He Cares. God continues His affirmation to Isaiah . . . *"and I will care for you"*. The apostle Peter gives a helpful word, *"Give all your worries and cares to God, for He cares about you."* (1 Pet 5:7 NLT). Some translations use the phrase, "casting your cares on Him". We often need to gather each care and every worry, ball them up in a blanket of His grace and throw them to the loving hands of God. He will unwrap, unravel and untangle all of our problems and give us peace.

He Will Carry. Our God not only saves, He sustains. Isaiah writes, *"I will carry you along and save you."* The psalmist tells us, *"Praise the Lord; praise God our Savior! For each day He carries us in His arms."* (Ps 68:19 NLT). Each day, He is there . . . never leaving us alone. He never abandons us.

Scott Wesley Brown writes the following encouraging lyrics,

> *"There is no problem too big*
> *God cannot solve it.*
> *There is no mountain too tall*
> *God cannot move it."*

"There is no storm too dark
God cannot calm it.
There is no sorrow too deep
He cannot soothe it."
"Oh, if He carries the weight of the world upon His shoulders,
I know my brother that He will carry you.
Oh, if He carries the weight of the world upon His shoulders,
I know my sister that He will carry you."[105]

It begins with letting go of everything else and grabbing on to Him.

Your Creator is committed to His process, He cares about you . . . and He will carry you.

KINGDOM THOUGHT 60: COURAGE

This is my command—be strong and courageous! Do not be afraid or discouraged. For the Lord your God is with you wherever you go.
Joshua 1:9 NLT

Courage is defined as "a quality of spirit that enables one to face danger or pain without surrendering to fear".

Giving into fear leads to discouragement . . . abandoning courage.

Giving into faith leads to encouragement . . . applying courage.

The psalmist reminds us, *"When I am afraid, I will put my trust in You."* (Ps 56:3 NASB)

In the writings of Joshua, the people of Israel had just come through a tragic and tremendous loss. Moses, their loving leader had passed. As a nation, their opportunities encountered overwhelming opposition. Any security or safety they may have felt could be stricken with struggling times. Joshua is now in charge, but he is anticipating great anxiety. God tells him to be strong and to have courage . . . but, also tells Joshua that he is not alone.

Courage In His Presence. You may recall the saying, "You and God always equal a majority". The presence of God gives us an overcoming advantage over the enemy of fear. God assures Joshua of His never leaving presence. Wherever Joshua goes, God is there. David reminds us that even when *"we walk through the valley of death's shadow"* (Ps 23), God is with us. The prophet Isaiah writes, *"Don't be afraid, for I am with you. Don't be discouraged, for I am your God. I will strengthen you and help you. I will hold you up with My victorious right hand."* (Is 41:10 NLT).

Our God is with us . . . through thick or thin . . . in good times or bad . . . He is always there.

Courage In His Purpose. God is always walking with us and He is always working in us. Paul reminds the believers in Philippi, *"And I am certain that God, who began the good work within you, will continue his work until it is finally finished on the day when Christ Jesus returns."* (Phil 1:6 NLT) Sometimes that means we carry a heavy load . . . but it's never a load too heavy. Reggie White says, "God places the heaviest burden on those who can carry its weight."[106]

God can be trusted in our trials and in our testing . . . through thick or thin . . . in good times or bad . . . He has a purpose and a plan for our good and His glory.

Courage In His Promises. Because God's promises are true, He can be trusted. God promises David that his son will build the temple. As the project begins, David reminds Solomon of God's promise, *"Be strong and courageous, and do the work. Don't be afraid or discouraged, for the Lord God, my God, is with you. He will not fail you or forsake you. He will see to it that all the work related to the Temple of the Lord is finished correctly."* (1 Chron 28:20 NLT). Paul tells us a very simple, yet significant statement, *"This truth gives them confidence that they have eternal life, which God—who does not lie—promised them before the world began."* (Titus 1:2 NLT).

We can have courage because of His promises . . . through thick or thin . . . in good times or bad . . . He will not fail or forsake . . . He will finish His promised work.

Clay Crosse writes the following lyrics,

> *"Fears like a black cloud consuming all that's blue.*
> *When I am afraid, I will trust in you.*
> *Waters rise against me and I don't know what to do.*
> *When I am afraid, I will trust in you."*
> *"When I am afraid, I will trust in you.*
> *Remind myself your faithful and your promises are true.*
> *I think back on my yesterdays and all you brought me through.*
> *When I am afraid, I will trust in you."*

Be encouraged . . . He is with you . . . He is working in you . . . He keeps His word.

KINGDOM THOUGHT 61: LAYERS

For of His fullness we have all received, and grace upon grace.
John 1:16 NASB

In the Chesapeake Bay area of Maryland, there is a dessert known as the Smith Island Cake. It's a six to twelve-layer yellow cake with old fashioned chocolate fudge frosting between each layer. It's a masterpiece. It's layer upon layer upon layer of goodness.

John tells us that we have received not just grace . . . but, grace layered on top of grace. The entomology means grace upon grace, upon grace, upon grace . . . an unending supply of grace. The source is the fullness of Jesus . . . The Savior for sinners who are made saints.

John Newton first called it "Amazing Grace".

Grace is the richness of Christ and the riches of Christ.

Grace is initiated in God's heart, imparted by His love and infused by faith.

Grace is something we don't deserve, yet desperately need.

Grace gives us power when we are weak, peace when we are troubled and purpose when we are aimless.

Grace is one of God's great gifts . . . we cannot earn it . . . we cannot work for it . . . we receive it. It's not about anything we have done . . . it's all about what God has done.

Saving Grace. A. W. Tozer writes, "The cross is the lightning rod of grace that short-circuits God's wrath to Christ so that only the light of His love remains for believers."[107] God's initial impact on our lives is grace that saves. It is His life gift that gives lasting acceptance. Paul writes, *"For by grace you have been saved through faith. And this is not your own doing; it is the gift of God, not a result of works, so that no one may boast."* (Eph 2:8-9 ESV)

Sustaining Grace. Grace that saves is eternal while grace that sustains is every day. It guarantees our salvation and guides us in our suffering. Peter reminds us, *"And after you have suffered a little while, the God of all grace, who has called you to his eternal glory in Christ, will Himself restore, confirm, strengthen, and establish you."* (1 Pet 5:10 ESV). God gives us a bold invitation to draw near and discover grace. The writer of Hebrews tells us, *"Let us then with confidence draw near to the throne of grace, that we may receive mercy and find grace to help in time of need."* (Heb 4:16 ESV)

Strengthening Grace. Grace is there when we are weak, weary and worn down. He is the help in our helplessness. Paul confesses, *"Three times I pleaded* *with the Lord about this, that it should leave me. But he said to me, 'My grace is sufficient for you, for my power is made perfect in weakness.' Therefore, I will boast all the more gladly of my weaknesses, so that the power of Christ may rest upon me."* (2 Cor12:8-9 ESV). We no longer hide our weaknesses . . . we reveal the power of His grace.

Abraham Lincoln said, "Intoxicated with unbroken success, we have become too self-sufficient to feel the necessity of redeeming and preserving grace, too proud to pray to the God that made us."[108]

Today, be defined, dependent and desperate for His saving, sustaining and strengthening grace . . . IT IS AMAZING!

KINGDOM THOUGHT 62: EARLY

And rising very early in the morning, while it was still dark, He departed and went out to a desolate place, and there He prayed.
Mark 1:35 ESV

People are always looking for easy steps to success. To some it may be a "hidden code", the "secret recipe" or the proverbial "secret sauce". In reality, there are no quick fixes. Good things may come to those who wait . . . but, while waiting they work hard. They pay the price . . . doing the little things well makes the big things work.

In the first chapter of Mark's Gospel, Jesus begins His public and profound ministry. He makes a difference. He does something big. Mark tells us, *"That evening at sundown they brought to Him all who were sick or oppressed by demons. And the whole city was gathered together at the door. And He healed many . . ."* (Mark 1:32-34 ESV). Notice the words . . . *"all who were sick or oppressed"* and *"the whole city".* Jesus draws a needy crowd . . . and, He meets their needs.

That kind of day would cause many of us to take the next day off. Exhaustion often leads to escape. The next verse uncovers the little thing that Jesus does well . . . the thing that helps Him refocus and replenish . . . He finds time with His Heavenly Father.

Sacrifice. Mark tells us, *"And rising very early in the morning, while it was still dark . . . ".* Before the daily demands, Jesus determines His direction. Getting up before dawn is a sacrifice worth making. The psalmist writes, *"O God, you are my God; earnestly I seek you; my soul thirsts for you; my flesh faints for you, as in a dry and weary land where there is no water."* (Ps 63:1 ESV). It's not so much a "specific" time . . . but a "sacred" time. It's a time that we will give up anything for and not give up for anything for it.

Solitude. Mark continues, *" . . . He departed and went out to a desolate place . . . ".* Although its inference is subtle, it is significant. Jesus separates Himself from the disciples . . . the people who need His attention and those who help Him . . . so He could be alone. The distractions in life can detour or derail us from our desired destination. Jesus reminds us, *"But when you pray, go away by yourself, shut the door behind you, and pray to your Father in private. Then your Father, who sees everything, will reward you."* (Matt 6:6 NLT) There are times when we must abandon ourselves to God, alone. No one else can help and He is our only hope.

Supplication. Mark writes, *" . . . and there He prayed."* The priority (sacrifice) and the place (solitude) are needed . . . but, the prayer (supplication) is necessary. Luke, the follower and physician reminds us, *"But Jesus often withdrew to the wilderness for prayer."* (Luke 5:16 NLT). When Jesus withdraws . . . He worships. It's often easier for us to review and plan than to rest in His presence and praise Him. Paul encourages us, *"Do not be anxious about anything, but in every situation, by prayer and petition, with thanksgiving, present your requests to God. And the peace of God, which transcends all understanding, will guard your hearts and your minds in Christ Jesus."* (Phil 4:6-7 NIV)

Corrie Ten Boom, a Dutch watchmaker and Christian whose family helped Jews escape Nazi persecution writes, "Don't pray when you feel like it. Have an appointment with the Lord and keep it. A man (or woman) is powerful on his knees."

So, here's the "secret sauce" . . . make it a priority to find a place and pray. It's a family recipe written by the Father, Himself.

KINGDOM THOUGHT 63: WHAT A GREAT GIFT

For the wages of sin is death, but the free gift of God is eternal life in Christ Jesus our Lord.
Romans 6:23 ESV

None of us likes to talk about sin. The result of sin is usually not the topic of choice at get togethers with friends or co-workers. However, there is a reality of sin. Sin is always tied to selfishness or self gone astray. Sin has a consequence. Sin always hurts someone . . . either others or ourselves.

From our perspective, sin is violating a standard or law. From God's perspective, it is that part in each of us . . . no matter how much effort we put in or how hard we try . . . nothing measures up to the eternal and Divine standard that, on our own, we cannot meet. The prophet Jeremiah writes, *"The heart is deceitful above all things, and desperately sick; who can understand it?"* (Jer 17:9 ESV). Paul reminds the followers in Rome, *"There are none righteous . . . no, not even one."* (Rom 3:23)

Although sin has a payment, God had a plan. Sin's consequence has been cancelled by God's compassion. Paul tells us that the result of "sin is death", but the "free gift of God is eternal life in Christ Jesus our Lord".

His Gift is Generous. We should be required to pay the "wages of sin", but instead we have a "free gift of God". God's generosity toward us comes at a considerable cost to Him. John writes, *"For God so loved the world, that he gave his only Son, that whoever believes in him should not perish but have eternal life. For God did not send his Son into the world to condemn the world, but in order that the world might be saved through him."* (John 3:16-17 ESV). God's love leads Him to give so that we might gain.

What generosity.

His Gift Is Gracious. No matter how hard we try, we can never dig ourselves out of sin's deep hole. The psalmist writes, *"He drew me up from the pit of destruction, out of the miry bog, and set my feet upon a rock, making my steps secure."* (Ps 40:2 ESV) God sees our mess and gave us mercy. This awesome gift is based on His amazing grace. Paul makes it clear to us, *"But God, being rich in mercy, because of the great love with which He loved us, even when we were dead in our trespasses, made us alive together with Christ—by grace you have been saved"* (Eph 2:4-5 ESV). In our lostness we are loved.

What generosity . . . What grace.

His Gift Is Glorious. The provision of God's extended grace is the promise of God's exemplified glory. This glory is seen in our everyday. Paul writes, *"For what is our hope, our joy, or the crown in which we will glory in the presence of our Lord Jesus when he comes? Is it not you? Indeed, you are our glory and joy."* (1 Thess 2:19-20 NIV). And, this glory is also our eternity. John writes, *"Dear friends, we are God's children, but He has not yet shown us what we will be like when Christ appears. But we do know that we will be like Him, for we will see Him as He really is. And all who have this eager expectation will keep themselves pure, just as He is pure."* (1 John 3:2-3 NLT). Through each day and in all eternity . . . we are His gifted and graceful glory.

What generosity . . . What grace . . . What a glory.

God is so generous that He gives His Son so we can be His children. His grace is an extension of His generous gift. And, He redeems us as His own for our good and His glory.

I like the way Eugene Peterson sums up these verses in The Message, *"Since we've compiled this long and sorry record as sinners and proved that we are utterly incapable of living the glorious lives God wills for us, God did it for us. Out of sheer generosity He put us in right standing with Himself. A pure gift. He got us out of the mess we're in and restored us to where He always wanted us to be. And, He did it by means of Jesus Christ."* (Rom 3:23-24 MSG)

The Apostle Paul gives us the next steps, *"If you openly declare that Jesus is Lord and believe in your heart that God raised him from the dead, you will be saved. For it is by believing in your heart that you are made right with God, and it is by openly declaring your faith that you are saved."* (Rom 10:9-10 NLT)

When we give our lives to Him, He gives life to us. God does it . . . for us!

KINGDOM THOUGHT 64: TO KNOW HIM

Yes, everything else is worthless when compared with the infinite value of knowing Christ Jesus my Lord. For His sake I have discarded everything else, counting it all as garbage, so that I could gain Christ.
Philippians 3:8 NLT

Intimacy intensifies intentions.

Remember those early days of dating and romance? The more time you spent with "the one", the more feelings deepened and developed.

The love of Christ and the longing to be like Him influenced the Apostle Paul to see everything else as wanting, deficient and lacking. Every detour, distraction or derailment had to go. His commitment to know Christ may cause discomfort but, it will clarify his destiny.

Our Priority. There is an *"infinite value of knowing Christ Jesus"*. A priority is something that is established based on importance or urgency. Paul's most pressing issue is to know Jesus. It is of utmost urgency. If we're going to abandon ourselves to Christ, we must be "all in". Through the prophet Jeremiah, God reminds us, *"You will seek me and find me when you seek me with all your heart."* (Jer 29:13 NIV). A transformed tax-collector records Jesus' teaching regarding priorities, *"But seek first His kingdom and His righteousness, and all these things will be given to you as well."* (Matt 6:33 NIV)

What gets you up in the morning? What's the first thought on your mind? What's the one thing you must do before you do anything else? (I know the answer is coffee . . . but, after that . . .)

Paul tells us . . . *"That I might know Him . . ."* (Phil 3:10)

Our Pain. No pain . . . No gain. I wish it weren't true, but most times it is. In serving the Lord, Paul suffered loss. Pain is part of the process. The author of Hebrews tells us, *"Although he was a Son, Jesus learned obedience through what he suffered"* (Heb 5:8 ESV). He also writes, *"For we do not have a high priest who is unable to sympathize with our weaknesses, but one who in every respect has been tempted as we are, yet without sin."* (Heb 4:15 ESV). Jesus was "without sin" yet He "learned obedience". Piper writes, *"So learning obedience does not mean switching from disobedience to obedience. It means growing deeper and deeper with God in the experience of obedience. It means experiencing depths of yieldedness to God that would not have been otherwise demanded."*[109] This is the significance of our suffering. This is the gain in our pain.

Our Purpose. In our ministries, businesses or organizations, we spend considerable time on writing a "mission statement" . . . carefully selected and crafted words that keep us laser-focused on our purpose. Paul's purpose is clear . . . Jesus is his goal . . . he wants to become more like Christ. David writes, *"Whom have I in heaven but you? And there is nothing on earth that I desire besides you."* (Ps 73:25 ESV).

Rhea Miller writes the following beloved lyrics, "Than to be a king of a vast domain or be held in sin's dread sway, I'd rather have Jesus than anything this world affords today."[110] Let me lose all that I am, all that I have, all that want to win Him.

Charles Spurgeon says, "They who dive in the sea of affliction bring up rare pearls."[111] What rare pearls does He have for you today? Dive deep and you will find God's treasure!

There is no other purpose . . . no other plan . . . no other priority . . . but to win . . . to gain . . . to know Christ.

KINGDOM THOUGHT 65: IT'S ALL GOOD

Thus, the heavens and the earth were finished, and all the host of them. And on the seventh day God finished His work that He had done, and He rested on the seventh day from all His work that He had done.
Genesis 2:1-2 ESV

Made in the image of God . . . we each share a uniqueness with Almighty God. He fashioned us after His form, with freedom, with fully functional thought and with forthright will. In his allegorical work, "Voyage To Venus", C. S. Lewis writes, "For the resemblance was, in its own fashion, infinite, so that almost you could wonder at finding no sorrows on his brow and no wounds in his hands and feet."[112] Man was originally created without sin, struggle or suffering.

Love, freedom, intellect, morality . . . all characteristics of our Creator. Each is detailed in our design. The psalmist tells us, *"You made all the delicate, inner parts of my body and knit me together in my mother's womb. Thank you for making me so wonderfully complex! Your workmanship is marvelous—how well I know it."* (Ps 139:13-14 NLT). We model our Maker

We Create. We have an ability and aptitude to be creative, whatever our job. Catherwood writes, "There is an amazing stability among garage mechanics, to whom every repair job is different, who meets the customer, who sees the job through, who has the satisfaction of putting the car on the road again."[113] Our skill sets us apart. Solomon teaches, *"Do you see a man skillful in his work? He will stand before kings; he will not stand before obscure men."* (Prov 22:29 ESV). Paul reminds us of the special and specific gifts given to each of us, *"In his grace, God has given us different gifts for doing certain things well . . ."* (Rom 12:6 NLT). We are the Creators' creations commissioned to create.

We Cultivate. We not only create, we also develop, build and cultivate. God's first instruction-initiated work, *"Then God blessed them and said, 'Be fruitful and multiply. Fill the earth and govern it. Reign over the fish in the sea, the birds in the sky, and all the animals that scurry along the ground.'"* (Gen 1:28 NLT). It's good to cultivate . . . to get your hands dirty in developing something. Our motivation is our Master-Designer. Paul teaches, "So, whether you eat or drink, or whatever you do, do all to the glory of God." (1 Cor 10:31 ESV). There is great delight in diligence. It's been said that we "are the CEO of our own personal and professional growth plan." Become the best at what you do. Solomon writes, *"Work hard and become a leader; be lazy and become a slave."* (Prov 12:24 NLT)

We Celebrate. At the conclusion of His creative work, God takes time to rest and celebrate . . . He says, "It is good". Nehemiah leads Israel to rebuild the walls of a destroyed Jerusalem. At the completion of their work, they celebrate the work and words of God. Nehemiah writes, *"So the people went away to eat and drink at a festive meal, to share gifts of food, and to celebrate with great joy because they had heard God's words and understood them."* (Neh 8:12 NLT). Jesus illustrates the celebration of completed work in a parable of faithful servants, *"The master was full of praise. 'Well done, my good and faithful servant. You have been faithful in handling this small amount, so now I will give you many more responsibilities. Let's celebrate together!'"* (Matt 25:21 NLT). Solomon reminds us that there is a time for everything, *"a time to break down, and a time to build up; a time to weep, and a time to laugh; a time to mourn, and a time to dance."* (Ecc 3:3-4 ESV). Work hard to win . . . and celebrate the wins.

Our work becomes our contribution.

Today is a day to design and create . . . to develop and cultivate . . . and, to delight and celebrate.

Take a moment to stop and to say, "It is good"!

KINGDOM THOUGHT 66: WE ARE

God is faithful, by Whom you were called into fellowship with His Son, Jesus Christ our Lord.
1 Corinthians 1:9 NET

In each of us, there is an emptiness that can only be filled by The Eternal One. In the mid-1600's, Blaise Pascal published the following thought in "Pensees", "There is a God-shaped vacuum in the heart of every person, and it can never be filled by any created thing. It can only be filled by God, made known through Jesus Christ."

Paul declares that God is faithful by filling the hole in each of us through fellowship with His Son.

We are accepted and appreciated because of God's compassion and the completed work of Christ.

We are recipients of God's grace; we receive His gifts and are released from guilt.

Purposes gained, passion is given, and a place in an eternal family is granted. Our empty becomes filled only by God.

We Are Graced. Paul writes, *"I always thank my God for you because of the grace of God that was given to you in Christ Jesus. For you were made rich in every way in him, in all your speech and in every kind of knowledge."* (1 Cor 1:4-5 NET). God's grace is a gift He grants for His glory and our good. We find a new beginning when we come to our end. A. W. Pink writes, "Just as the sinner's despair of any hope from himself is the first prerequisite of a sound conversion, so the loss of all confidence in himself is the first essential in the believer's growth in grace."[114]

We Are Gifted. God's grace provides us with giftedness to impact others. Paul writes, "Even as the testimony about Christ was confirmed among you— so that you are not lacking in any gift, as you wait for the revealing of our Lord Jesus Christ." (1 Cor 1:6-7 ESV). These gifts are from the hand of God to help those in need. James reminds us of their source and significance. *"Every good gift and every perfect gift is from above, and cometh down from the Father of lights, with whom is no variableness, neither shadow of turning."* (Jam 1:17 KJV). And, God does not practice "use it or lose it". He never takes back or takes away. Paul tells the followers in Rome, *"For God's gifts and His call can never be withdrawn."* (Rom 11:29 NLT)

We Are Guiltless. God's merciful grace removes all of our guilt. *"Who will sustain you to the end, guiltless in the day of our Lord Jesus Christ."* (1 Cor 1:8 ESV). Paul reminds us, "There is therefore now no condemnation for those who are in Christ Jesus." (Rom 8:1 ESV). The price is paid, and peace is ours through Christ. Sin's shackles are severed. Guilt no longer grasps. We are free.

God extends each of us a call that He longs for us to accept so He can fill any vacuum in our soul . . . answer it.

Rest in His grace . . . use the gifts He gives . . . and, be free from the guilt of your past.

He is faithful!

KINGDOM THOUGHT 67: THROUGH HIM

In this the love of God was made manifest among us, that God sent his only Son into the world, so that we might live through Him.
1 John 4:9 ESV

God's love is initiating, inviting and impacting.

He reaches out to us, requests our presence and radically changes our lives.

And, because His love is made known, we are able to know Him and make Him known.

God sent His Son so we could not only be saved in eternity and from our sin . . . but, also from ourselves. Only our surrender to Jesus gives us the strength to live in Jesus. Living through Christ is not vicarious, but victorious.

Live Through Him. Paul reminds us, "My old self has been crucified with Christ. It is no longer I who live, but Christ lives in me. So, I live in this earthly body by trusting in the Son of God, who loved me and gave himself for me." (Gal 2:20 NLT). Trusting God gives us freedom from fear and failure. A. W. Tozer writes, "In almost everything that touches our everyday life on earth, God is pleased when we're pleased. He wills that we be as free as birds to soar and sing our maker's praise without anxiety."[115]

Love Through Him. The love of God moves us from fixating on self to focusing on others. Paul reminds the believers in Corinth, *"For the love of Christ controls us, since we have concluded this, that Christ died for all; therefore all have died. And he died for all so that those who live should no longer live for themselves but for him who died for them and was raised."* (2 Cor 5:14-15 NET). What we gain from God, we give to others. The apostle John writes, *"We know what real love is because Jesus gave up his life for us. So, we also ought to give up our lives for our brothers and sisters. If someone has enough money to live well and sees a brother or sister in need but shows no compassion—how can God's love be in that person?"* (1 Jn 3:16-17 NLT)

Lose Through Him. This is where faith walking can be a bit confusing . . . in Christ, we live in a principle of paradox . . . to be great, we must serve . . . to live, we must die . . . in success, we suffer. These are characteristics of God's Kingdom. One confusing concept is that we lose to gain. This is illustrated in the book of Philippians as Paul writes, *"Yes, everything else is worthless when compared with the infinite value of knowing Christ Jesus my Lord. For His sake I have discarded everything else, counting it all as garbage, so that I could gain*

Christ" (Phil 3:8 NLT) In God's economy, when we release, we receive. It's in the letting go that we learn grace. Only in total surrender do we find true satisfaction.

Our ability to serve is linked to our availability to surrender. We are reminded, *"I can do all things through Christ who empowers me"*. (Phil 4:13). This is a steady process of growth and grace. Billy Graham said, "Being a Christian is more than just an instantaneous conversion - it is a daily process whereby you grow to be more and more like Christ."[116]

Live . . . Love . . . Lose . . . and do it through Jesus.

KINGDOM THOUGHT 68: BRIDGE BUILDING

May the God of endurance and encouragement grant you to live in such harmony with one another, in accord with Christ Jesus.
Romans 15:5 ESV

Finding opportunities in our obstacles is founded by our observations of God.

As Paul writes to the Christ followers in Rome, he encourages the strong to help the struggling, the well to help the weary, and the faithful to help the fallen. He models his message of ministry after the Master's life. Paul explains the example of Jesus as One who endures and encourages.

God Our Example. Paul writes, *"For even Christ didn't live to please Himself. As the Scriptures say, 'The insults of those who insult you, O God, have fallen on me.'"* (Rom 15:3 NLT). Jesus gives us an example to embrace. Give. Serve. Love. The apostle reminds us, *"Imitate God, therefore, in everything you do, because you are His dear children. Live a life filled with love, following the example of Christ. He loved us and offered himself as a sacrifice for us, a pleasing aroma to God."* (Eph 5:1-2 NLT)

God Of Endurance. The writer of Hebrews recalls that this life is a race and running requires us to *"strip off every weight that slows us down, especially the sin that so easily trips us up."* (Heb 12:1 NLT). We are to *"run with endurance the race God has set before us."* We keep our *"eyes on the prize"* . . . we stay focused on Jesus because *"He endured the cross".* (Heb 12:2 NLT) When God becomes our example of endurance, we become committed to completing the course. In every opportunity, there are obstacles and opposition. Henry Ford said, "When everything seems to be going against you, remember that the airplane takes off against the wind, not with it."[117] We press on past fatigue and failure as we pursue in faith. The author of Hebrews instructs us, *"Think of all the hostility He (Jesus) endured from sinful people; then you won't become weary and give up."* (Heb 12:3 NLT)

God Of Encouragement. The psalmist reminds us that God's Word is a lamp and light in our journey. (Ps 119:105) Paul tells the believers in Rome that, *"Scriptures give us hope and encouragement as we wait patiently for God's promises to be fulfilled."* (Rom 15:4 NLT) God's promises give us hope and God's presence gives us help. Sharing God's hope and help brings harmony. Paul writes, *"He comforts us in all our troubles so that we can comfort others. When they are troubled, we will be able to give them the same comfort God has given us".* (2 Cor 1:4 NLT). Encouragement can energize our efforts . . . discouragement can destroy our dreams. Abraham Lincoln said, "Let no feeling of discouragement prey upon you, and in the end you are sure to succeed."[118]

God gives us an example . . . He gives us endurance . . . He encourages us. He asks that we do the same for others.

There's a lyric that reads, "You can build a wall, or you can build a bridge. It all depends upon the love you give. If you build a wall, your world is small. But, a bridge of love will conquer all."[119]

Let's build a bridge of encouragement that will endure and be an example to all.

Kingdom Thought 69: I Can Live With That

In Him we were also chosen, having been predestined according to the plan of Him who works out everything in conformity with the purpose of His will, in order that we, who were the first to put our hope in Christ, might be for the praise of His glory.
Ephesians 1:11-12 NIV

During a troubling time, several years ago, one of our daughters wrote, "A month ago, my world was being turned upside down. I was in a place of fear, hurt and anxiety. I wanted to trust Jesus, but it's easier said than done."

I've been there . . . what am I saying . . . I am usually there.

We know Jesus is worthy of our trust and we want to give it to Him . . . but, being willing to take those steps of surrender . . . that's tough.

But that's when our faith overtakes fear, our hope heals hurt, and our abandonment to Him replaces anxiety.

The apostle Paul reminds us that Jesus chooses us . . . and His choice gives us confidence and conviction in Him.

His Plan. My understanding of God's unique plan has expanded over the years. The psalmist writes, "Many, Lord my God, are the wonders You have done, the things You planned for us. None can compare with You; were I to speak and tell of Your deeds, they would be too many to declare." (Ps 40:5 NIV). God's plan illustrates the grace, growth and gifts that He gives each of us. The prophet Jeremiah reminds exiled Israel of God's strategy, even in the middle of their suffering. He writes, "For I know the plans I have for you, declares the Lord, plans for welfare and not for evil, to give you a future and a hope." (Jer 29:11 ESV). His plan is based on His wisdom, His understanding and His insight.

His Purpose. Paul encourages us that God's plan fulfills His purpose, *"according to the plan of Him who works out everything in conformity with the purpose of His will."* (Eph 1:11). We often equate success with being in the center of God's will and fulfilling His purpose for our lives. Rick Warren writes, "Being successful and fulfilling your life's purpose are not at all the same thing; You can reach all your personal goals, become a raving success by the worlds standard and still miss your purpose in this life."[120] Paul shares his perspective on God's purpose, *"I once thought these things were valuable, but now I consider them worthless because of what Christ has done. Yes, everything else is worthless when compared with the infinite value of knowing Christ Jesus my Lord. For His sake I have discarded everything else, counting it all as garbage, so that I could gain Christ and become one with Him. I no longer count on my own righteousness* *through obeying the law; rather, I become righteous through faith in Christ. For God's way of making us right with himself depends on faith."* (Phil 3:7-9 NLT). It's not what we accomplish or what we attain . . . it's Who we adore. Bottom line . . . God wants us to know Him and to make Him known.

His Praise. It's all about His praise. God's glory is the goal. Jesus says, "In the same way, let your light shine before others, so that they may see your good works and give glory to your Father Who is in heaven." (Matt 5:16 ESV). When we recognize God's grace, He receives the glory. His plan and purpose is evident in everything. Paul reminds the Christ-followers in Corinth, "So, whether you eat or drink, or whatever you do, do all to the glory of God." (1 Cor 10:31 ESV)

Our daughter finished her thoughts, "Today, I can honestly say without reserve that I serve a faithful God (something I've always believed in my head, but my heart sometimes lacked)."

Our renewed hope comes when the perception in our head moves to the practice of our heart. For some of us, that's a long journey.

His plan and His purpose . . . all for His praise. I can live with that.

Kingdom Thought 70: Who Over What

And this righteousness will bring peace. Yes, it will bring quietness and confidence forever.
Isaiah 32:17 NLT

Sadly, it's easier to raise a generation to believe that righteousness or right living is founded on what we do, instead of who we are.

Righteousness based on what we do becomes rule driven and unwelcoming.

Righteousness based in who we are becomes relationship driven and inviting.

Right living moves from the inside out, not from the outside in.

What we do is evaluated in goodness.

Who we are is established in grace.

A greater challenge is raising a generation which embraces that we all are unrighteous only made righteous by the grace, mercy and love of God's Righteous Son. Paul reminds us, *"For God made Christ, who never sinned, to be the offering for our sin, so that we could be made right with God through Christ."* (2 Cor 5:21 NLT)

The prophet Isaiah foretells of this kind of righteous living provided by a Righteous King whose Kingdom is not of this world and lasts forever. This kind of righteousness is founded in the "Who" and not the "what".

This Kind Of Righteousness Brings Peace. There is a *"peace that surpasses all understanding"* and *"it guards our hearts and minds"* . . . it protects our feelings and thoughts . . . *"in Christ Jesus".* (Phil 4:6-7). Jesus says, *"I have told you all this so that you may have peace in me. Here on earth you will have many trials and sorrows. But take heart, because I have overcome the world."* (John 16:33 NLT). Peace is only found in our Prince of Peace. C. S. Lewis writes, "God cannot give us a happiness and peace apart from Himself, because it is not there. There is no such thing."[121]

Righteousness brings peace.

This Kind Of Righteousness Brings Quietness. I do not live in a world of quietness. Having ten grandchildren creates more rejoicing chaos than relaxing calm. The quietness illustrated by Isaiah is a quietness of heart before an Almighty God. In the demands of a growing crowd, Jesus instructs His disciples, *"Let's go off by ourselves to a quiet place and rest awhile."* (Mark 6:31 NLT). It's in stillness that our struggles find a solution. The psalmist tells us God's invitation, *"Be still, and know that I am God."* (Ps 46:10 ESV). We have a Holy God reaching out to a hopeless man.

Righteousness brings quietness.

This Kind Of Righteousness Brings Confidence. If we base our relationship with God is based on what we do, we flounder in a world of failure. If our rightness before God is based on who we are in Him, we flourish in our faith. Paul tells us, *"There is therefore now no condemnation for those who are in Christ Jesus."* (Rom 8:1 ESV). Even in uncertain times, we can have unwavering confidence in Him. Solomon writes, *"Do not be afraid of sudden terror or of the ruin of the wicked, when it comes, for the Lord will be your confidence and will keep your foot from being caught."* (Prov 3:25-26 ESV).

Righteousness brings confidence.

God makes us right. Our being takes precedent over our doing. What's on the inside overshadows what's on the outside.

He is Peace to your problems.

He is calm to your chaos.

He is certainty in your uncertainty.

His gifts and grace are not just for today . . . they are forever.

This is the kind of righteousness that we want . . . that we need . . . and, that we have in Jesus.

KINGDOM THOUGHT 71: SHE'S THE BEST

Who can find a virtuous and capable wife? She is more precious than rubies.
Proverbs 31:10 NLT

The inspired writer of Proverbs asks one of the most important and impacting questions of life . . . *"Who can find an amazing wife?"*

The "find" involves intentional searching, that once completed offers a life of immeasurable satisfaction.

The parameters of the search often become skewed. Many look for "the one" who will check off all the boxes on their list. Too many times, the initial search does not take into account the invested seasoning of a relationship. Sadly, too many give up too soon on growing together.

Some trade in the tried and true for a new trophy. Errors are exaggerated. Faults or failures are not forgiven. Hurts are not healed.

Building a relationship is not about perfection . . . it's about passion, patience, purpose and priorities.

The choice is critical.

Her Virtue. The wise author of Proverbs comments on the valued woman, *"She opens her arms to the poor and extends her hands to the needy." (*Prov 31:20 NIV). A virtuous woman has a heart for those in need and helps with her deeds. John describes this giving grace and meaningful mercy, *"If anyone has material possessions and sees a brother or sister in need but has no pity on them, how can the love of God be that person? Dear children, let us not love with words or speech but with actions and in truth."* (1 John 3:17-18 NIV). This prized woman cares for her family and has compassion for those suffering misfortunes, both economically and emotionally. Her heart is tender and often touched.

Her Value. Proverbs describes this woman as *"more precious than rubies"*. Gemstones are valued because of their rareness and intrinsic beauty. Commonness is not costly . . . but worthiness is the highest wealth. Passion for her everyday and purpose for eternity are her treasures. The resolute meaning of her life is reflected in marriage, mothering and mentoring. This virtuous woman is valued by her spouse. *"She brings him good, not harm, all the days of her life."* (Prov 31:12 NIV) Martin Luther said of his wife, "The greatest gift of God is a pious amiable spouse, who fears God, loves his house, and with whom one can live in perfect confidence."[122]

Her Vision. The virtuous woman's choices give her confidence for the future. There is no terror for tomorrow. Proverbs reminds us, *"She is clothed with strength and dignity; she can laugh at the days to come."* (Prov 31:25 NIV). Bridges writes, "Having been so wisely provident for the morrow, she is not overburdened with its cares."[123] This woman has the certainty that God will complete what He has conceived. Paul reminds us, *"And I am certain that God, Who began the good work within you, will continue His work until it is finally finished on the day when Christ Jesus returns."* (Phil 1:6 NLT). She rests in her Redeemer.

This woman is the epitome of grace. Grace is never earned. Grace is never deserved. Grace requires growth.

Almost 40 years ago, I married a woman who lives these virtues. She is a . . .

. . . giver of grace,

. . . patient partner,

. . . magnificent mother,

. . . generous grandy,

. . . exceptional entrepreneur,

. . . compassionate coach,

. . . masterful mentor,

. . . terrific teacher,

. . . faithful friend, and

. . . wonderful woman.

Eugene Peterson, in his paraphrasing work, The Message says it well, *"Charm can mislead, and beauty soon fades. The woman to be admired and praised is the woman who lives in the Fear of God. Give her everything she deserves! Festoon her life with praises!"* (Proverbs 31:30-31 MSG)

I am blessed to have found my treasured and valuable gem. Her radiance still shines.

KINGDOM THOUGHT 72: PAY BACK

See that no one pays back evil for evil, but always try to do good to each other and to all people.
1 Thessalonians 5:15 NLT

The teaching of Jesus pierces through the darkness of pious religious tradition and politically revengeful tyranny.

During His time, the Jews promoted guilt and piety, while the Romans perfected guile and politics. Today, it is common practice to "chew someone out" or "eat them alive". American novelist Alfred Hitchcock wrote, "Revenge is sweet and not fattening."[124]

Paul shares a different thought. With a foundation of grace and goodness, he teaches Jesus' truth of reconciliation and not revenge, good instead of evil, compassion instead of condemnation. Many in the first century were impacted by this influence. Roman General Marcus Aurelius wrote, "The best revenge is to be unlike him who performed the injury."[125]

Say No To Paying It Back. In his closing comments to the Thessalonians, Paul insists that responses between rivals be no longer evil. Pay back is no longer an option. As Christ followers, it's time to get over getting even. Moses writes in Israel's legal code, *"Do not seek revenge or bear a grudge against a fellow Israelite but love your neighbor as yourself. I am The Lord."* (Lev 19:18 NLT). Our responses are in respect, not in retaliation . . . they are honorable, not hurtful. In his letter to believers in Rome, Paul writes, *"Repay no one evil for evil, but give thought to do what is honorable in the sight of all."* (Rom 12:17 ESV). This kind of avenging is rooted in anger. We are reminded, *"anger gives a foothold to the devil."* (Eph 4:27 NLT).

Revenge and retaliation are not our response.

Say Yes To Paying It Forward. Full compensation for revenge requires a different kind of currency. Instead of paying back with evil, we are to pay forward with good. Paul reminds us, *"If possible, so far as it depends on you, live peaceably with all."* (Rom 12:18 ESV). Jesus gives a new instruction, *"But I say, love your enemies! Pray for those who persecute you!"* (Matt 5:44 NLT) Martin Luther King, Jr. writes. "Man must evolve for all human conflict a method which rejects revenge, aggression and retaliation. The foundation of such a method is love."[126] This kind of response extends to our circle of friends and to our community in full. Peter reminds us of the benefit of blessing, *"Do not repay evil with evil or insult with insult. On the contrary, repay evil with blessing, because to this you were called so that you may inherit a blessing."* (1 Pet 3:9 NIV).

Goodness and grace are our response.

God's grace is evidenced when goodness is extended.

God blesses us when we bless others.

God's light shines when we show His love.

So today, instead of giving someone a piece of our mind . . . let's give them a place in our heart.

KINGDOM THOUGHT 73: TWO EARS ONE MOUTH

Understand this, my dear brothers and sisters: You must all be quick to listen, slow to speak, and slow to get angry.
James 1:19 NLT

Ever wondered why one mouth is twice as hurtful as two ears are helpful? One mouth . . . two ears . . . yet, most of us only listen half as much as talk.

James, the brother of Jesus writes his letter to first century Christ followers giving practical and insightful advice for living an influential and impacting life. He finds an undeniable link between our readiness to listen and our resulting necessity to speak. If we do one, we can't do the other. And, if we master hearing, we minimize hostility.

Quick To Listen. We often lean in to listen. It becomes our initial and intuitive response. We are ready and willing to open our ears. Earnest Hemingway says, "I like to listen. I have learned a great deal from listening carefully. Most people never listen."[127] Solomon links listening to wise living. He writes, *"Fools think their own way is right, but the wise listen to others."* (Prov 12:15 NLT). Keeping a reign on the rambling can result in a reputation of reasoning. The wise king writes, *"Even a fool who keeps silent is considered wise; when he closes his lips, he is deemed intelligent."* (Prov 17:28 ESV) Jesus teaches the value of listening and learning, *"Everyone then who hears these words of mine and does them will be like a wise man who built his house on the rock."* (Matt 7:24 ESV)

Slow To Speak. A. D. Williams said, "Words have special powers . . . to lift up or put down . . . to heal or harm. Choose your words carefully."[128] Wandering words can lead to waste or wreck. Solomon writes, *"Too much talk leads to sin. Be sensible and keep your mouth shut."* (Prov 10:19 NLT). We often think that telling others how to live gives them a meaningful life. But, James reminds us, *"If you claim to be religious but don't control your tongue, you are fooling yourself, and your religion is worthless."* (Jam1:26 NLT)

Slower To Anger. Quickness to anger quenches our peace. Ralph Waldo Emerson explains, "For every minute you remain angry, you give up sixty seconds of peace of mind."[129] Anger has a destructive and demoralizing effect. It is described as a raging fire that consumes everything in its path. American satirist Mark Twain says, "Anger is an acid that can do more harm to the vessel in which it is stored than to anything on which it is poured."[130] Losing it can label us. Solomon is direct in his advice, *"Control your temper, for anger labels you a fool."* (Ecc 7:9 NLT).

Frank Tyger reminds us, "Be a good listener. Your ears will never get you in trouble."[131]

Eugene Peterson in "The Message" give some thoughts on this verse, *"Post this at all the intersections, dear friends: Lead with your ears, follow up with your tongue, and let anger straggle along in the rear."* (James 1:19 MSG)

Two ears . . . One mouth. Two keep us from trouble . . . one gets us into it.

KINGDOM THOUGHT 74: WHAT GOD EXPECTS

No, O people, the LORD has told you what is good, and this is what He requires of you: to do what is right, to love mercy, and to walk humbly with your God.
Micah 6:8 NLT

I can't tell you how many times I struggle with the questions, "Am I doing any good?" or "Am I pleasing God?" The prophet Micah gives instruction to the nations of what pleases God. It's not sacrifice, but the heart behind the sacrifice. Our attitudes drive our actions.

So, what is right and what does God require? The prophet gives us some insight.

Do What Is Right. Solomon shares, *"To do what is right and just is more acceptable to the LORD than sacrifice."* (Prov 21:3) Doing what is right promotes the passion, purpose and principles of God. When we honor Him, we please Him. Leonard Ravenhill writes, "If we displease God, does it matter whom we please? If we please Him does it matter whom we displease?"[132] Our doing starts with our being. Paul reminds us, *"And now, dear brothers and sisters, one final thing. Fix your thoughts on what is true, and honorable, and right, and pure, and lovely, and admirable. Think about things that are excellent and worthy of praise."* (Phil 4:8 NLT)

Love Mercy. When you love something, you want to share it. Mercy is defined as, "compassion or forgiveness shown toward someone whom it is within one's power to punish or harm." Abraham Lincoln writes, "I have always found that mercy bears richer fruits than strict justice."[133] The prophet Hosea reminds us of the magnificence of showing mercy. He shares, *"For I desire mercy, not sacrifice, and acknowledge of God rather than burnt offerings."* (Hosea 6:6) Loving mercy is illustrated in our initial response to injustice . . . in our societies, our communities and our homes.

Mercy is a healing salve in our hurting struggles.

Mercy is compassion in our conflicts.

Mercy is grace in our grief.

Love mercy . . . show mercy . . . give mercy.

Walk Humbly With God. James reminds us, *"Humble yourselves before the Lord, and He will lift you up."* (James 4:10 NIV) Humility is seeing ourselves as God sees us . . . significant enough to experience His mercy, grace and love . . . yet willing to serve to express His mercy, grace and love. David Wells writes,

"Humility has nothing to do with depreciating ourselves and our gifts in ways we know to be untrue. Even 'humble' attitudes can be masks of pride. Humility is that freedom from our self which enables us to be in positions in which we have neither recognition nor importance, neither power nor visibility, and even experience deprivation, and yet have joy and delight. It is the freedom of knowing that we are not in the center of the universe, not even in the center of our own private universe."[134] Don't settle on seeing yourself the way others see you . . . be satisfied with the way God sees you . . . worthy, willing and His workmanship.

Walking with God requires our communion with Him, our commitment to Him and our confidence in Him.

Walk well, my friends . . . walk well.

KINGDOM THOUGHT 75: LET GO

He gives power to the weak and strength to the powerless.
Isaiah 40:29

There are days when being weary, weak and worn out starts to win out . . . and, giving in, giving up or giving out seems to be the only way.

We face challenges every day. Some are small and some are staggering.

As we face these, some say we should be "committed to the cause".

As God looks at us, He says we should be "surrendered to the Savior".

There's a dividing difference between commitment and surrender.

Commitment is dependent on my determination, my dedication and my drive. It's me getting up.

Surrender is relinquishing my rights, my responsibilities and my resources. It's me giving in.

Commitment means I'm doing the work. Surrender means He's doing the work in me.

Commitment says, "No matter what, I can." Surrender says, "No matter what, I can't."

Commitment relies on strength. Surrender rests in weakness.

Commitment alone is lacking. Surrendering my commitment to God is lasting.

A. W. Tozer writes, "The reason why many are still troubled, still seeking, still making little forward progress is because they haven't yet come to the end of themselves. We're still trying to give orders and interfering with God's work within us."[135]

Isaiah understands the efforts and the emptiness of our own interference. He instructs us that God is there for those who are worn out and He is there for those who are weak.

Renewed Strength For The Weary. Some have been in battle so long that their determination has been depleted. It may be hard to grasp, but this is exactly where God wants us. A few verses later, Isaiah reminds us, *"but those who hope in the LORD will renew their strength."* (Is 40:31 NIV) Our God comes along side to renew and refresh when all strength is gone. Paul encourages us, *"So we do not lose heart. Though our outer self is wasting away, our inner self is being renewed day by day."* (2 Cor 4:16 ESV)

Surrender your weariness to His renewing strength.

New Strength For The Weak. Some never engaged in the battle because they have no strength. Fear or failure have paralyzed many into escaping, instead of engaging. Paul writes, *"For God has not given us a spirit of fearfulness, but one of power, love, and sound judgment."* (2 Tim 1:7 HCSB) If you are powerless, God will give you power. The apostle writes to the Christ followers in Philippi, *"I can do all things through Christ who empowers me."* (Phil 4:13)

Surrender your weakness to His new strength.

There are times when we don't know what to do, we don't know what to say, we don't know where to go or we don't know what to think . . . I've been there . . . I'm usually there.

Tommy Walker writes the following lyrics,

> *"When I don't know what to do, I'll lift my hands.*
> *When I don't know what to say, I'll speak Your praise.*
> *When I don't know where to go, I'll run to Your throne.*
> *When I don't know what to think, I'll stand on Your truth.*
> *When I don't know what to do, Lord, I surrender all."*[136]

All to Jesus, we surrender. Let go and let God.

KINGDOM THOUGHT 76: GIVING IT ALL

There is no greater love than to lay down one's life for one's friends.
John 15:13 NLT

So often we are lifting ourselves up and getting credit instead of laying our lives down and giving compassion.

The apostle Paul reminds us, *"If I gave everything I have to the poor and even sacrificed my body, I could boast about it; but if I didn't love others, I would have gained nothing."* (1 Cor 13:3 NLT)

Great love usually involves a great loss.

True freedom does not take lives by terror . . . true freedom willingly gives life for good. Freedom is not free . . . in the kingdoms of this earth or in the Kingdom of Heaven.

No Greater Service. Love cannot be defined or described apart from serving. It's not about what we can get, but what we can give. John F. Kennedy said, "My fellow Americans, ask not what your country can do for you, ask what you can do for your country."[137] This kind of love is marked by humility, hope and help for others. Paul writes, *"Love is patient and kind. Love is not jealous or boastful or proud or rude. It does not demand its own way. It is not irritable, and it keeps no record of being wronged. It does not rejoice about injustice but rejoices whenever the truth wins out. Love never gives up, never loses faith, is always hopeful, and endures through every circumstance."* (1 Cor 13:4-7 NLT)

No Greater Submission. Authentic love surrenders its own gratification through submission to a greater good. Jesus says, *"For I have come down from heaven to do the will of God who sent me, not to do my own will."* (John 6:38 NLT) The greatest good is the Glory of God. And, another good is the gift of being free. Joseph Campbell writes, "A hero is someone who has given his or her life to something bigger than oneself."[138] Sacrificing our own comforts for a greater cause . . . that's the submission of a soldier.

No Greater Sacrifice. John tells of Jesus' sacrifice and our required service, *"This is how we know what love is: Jesus Christ laid down his life for us. And we ought to lay down our lives for our brothers and sisters."* (1 John 3:16 NIV) There is no greater love . . . there is no higher calling. Bob Riley reminds us, "I have long believed that sacrifice is the pinnacle of patriotism."

Those who give everything create divine moments for all.

James Bryce says, "Patriotism consists not in waving the flag, but in striving that our country shall be righteous as well as strong."[139]

There is no greater love than that found in service, submission and sacrifice.

All are required.

All are right.

All must be remembered.

To those who have given all . . . thank you.

KINGDOM THOUGHT 77: SERVING OR SWERVING

Don't push your way to the front; don't sweet-talk your way to the top. Put yourself aside, and help others get ahead. Don't be obsessed with getting your own advantage. Forget yourselves long enough to lend a helping hand.
Philippians 2:3-4 MSG

In his paraphrased work, Eugene Peterson illustrates Paul's description of two choices . . . two clear options that focus on our own way or on the way of others . . . on self or on serving. The apostle gives an example of Jesus' surrender, submission and service. Paul instructs that we embrace the "mind of Christ" as we engage those around us.

This strategy requires us to set aside self and serve. Our promoting and positioning give way to a passion for and priority of others.

Self-Promotion. The struggle of our soul is to be selfless. Faith requires a fight against the flesh . . . saying no to us and yes to others. Paul writes, *"Don't be selfish; don't try to impress others. Be humble, thinking of others as better than yourselves."* (Phil 2:3 NLT). Thinking of others before we think of ourselves is the key to kindness. Matthew Henry reminds us, "Kindness is the law of Christ's kingdom".[140] Promoting self always means we prioritize self. Rick Joyner writes, "We can build influence by self-promotion, but God will only promote those who do not promote themselves. That which is built on self-promotion will have to be maintained by human striving."[141]

Self-Positioning. The apostle gives some advice, *"Don't look out only for your own interests, but take an interest in others, too."* (Phil 2:4 NLT). Seeing with clarity and compassion starts with viewing others through God's eyes. Brown writes, "Instead of fixing your eyes on those points in which you excel, fix them on those in which your neighbor excels you: this is true 'humility'." Positioning others ahead of ourselves promotes peace. The writer of Hebrews reminds us, *"Make every effort to live in peace with everyone and to be holy; without holiness no one will see the Lord."* (Heb 12:14 NIV)

Cheryl Bachelder, former CEO of Popeye's Chicken gives some simple, yet significant thoughts in her book, "Dare to Serve" . . .

"As a leader, the most ambitious thing you will ever attempt is removing yourself from the spotlight."

"Followers appreciate humble leaders - leaders with the ability to admit mistakes, to apologize, and to be vulnerable in difficult circumstances; leaders who think of others more than themselves."

"Leaders who serve others have three core values: human dignity, personal responsibility, and humility."

"Ambition is a problem if it is all about you."

"Other-focused leadership inspires people to thrive.

"Self-focused leadership induces people to survive."[142]

Saint Francis gives us the following prayer of selflessness . . .

> *"Lord, make me an instrument of your peace,*
> *Where there is hatred, let me sow love;*
> *Where there is injury, pardon;*
> *Where there is doubt, faith;*
> *Where there is despair, hope;*
> *Where there is darkness, light;*
> *Where there is sadness, joy.*
> *O Divine Master, grant that I may not so much seek to be consoled, as to console; to be understood, as to understand; to be loved, as to love.*
> *For it is in giving that we receive.*
> *It is in pardoning that we are pardoned, and it is in dying that we are born to Eternal Life."*[143]

Let's be identified by serving instead of self.

KINGDOM THOUGHT 78: AND, MY ANSWER IS

A gentle answer deflects anger, but harsh words make tempers flare.
Proverbs 15:1 NLT

Words are powerful.

The carefully chosen word can calm conflict.

The wrecking word can wage war.

Words can hurt or heal.

They can agitate or they can appease.

Pearl Strachan Hurd says, "Handle them carefully, for words have more power than atom bombs." [144]

King Solomon, noted as one of the wisest men who ever lived, encourages us to use a gentle response when anger rages. With a decisively chosen word we can divert danger. Our objective becomes disarming anger before it becomes destructive.

It's being as "cool as a cucumber" and not "blowing your stack". A few verses later, Solomon reminds us, *"A hot-tempered man stirs up strife, but he who is slow to anger quiets contention."* (Prov 15:18 ESV). The more heated an argument, the more harsh our words can be.

We work toward a response instead of a reaction.

A Good Answer. The wise king reminds us, *"The right word at the right time is like a custom-made piece of jewelry".* (Prov 25:11 MSG). The good word is like "apples of gold in settings of silver". Choosing the correct word with a calm mind is our best consideration. Abraham Lincoln insightfully states, "I am very little inclined on any occasion to say anything unless I hope to produce some good by it."[145] It is a good word, not a grieving word. It is an answer of restoration and not rejection. Once words are used, they can't be undone. Jodi Picoult writes, "Words are like eggs dropped from great heights; you can no more call them back than ignore the mess they leave when they fall."[146]

A Gracious Answer. Ann Voskamp tells us, "Anger is contagious. So is grace."[147] Paul reminds us, *"Let your conversation be gracious and attractive so that you will have the right response for everyone."* (Col 4:6 NLT). Words of grace are words of goodness. As recipients of grace we are to reflect grace . . . in our walk, in our ways and in our words. Solomon writes, *"Gracious words are like a honeycomb, sweetness to the soul and health to the body."* (Prov 16:24 ESV)

A Gentle Answer. Gill explains, "Mild words, gentle expressions, delivered with kindness and tenderness, humility and submission; these will work upon a man's passions, weaken his resentments, and break and scatter the storm of wrath raised in his breast."[148] A gentle word brings good wellness. Proverbs tells us, *"Gentle words are a tree of life; a deceitful tongue crushes the spirit."* (Prov 15:4 NLT). Life giving words leave a lasting legacy of love.

James gives some very constructive comments, *"If someone thinks he is religious yet does not bridle his tongue, and so deceives his heart, his religion is futile."* (Jam 1:26 NET). The psalmist grasps the great responsibility of good, gracious and gentle words. He writes, *"Set a guard, O Lord, over my mouth; keep watch over the door of my lips!"* (Ps 141:3 ESV)

Good and gentle words of grace . . . Oh, God, guard what we say.

Kingdom Thought 79: Look Behind the Curtain

As for you, you meant evil against me, but God meant it for good, to bring it about that many people should be kept alive, as they are today.
Genesis 50:20 ESV

Trusting God is sometimes hard . . . trusting people who are "God's messengers" in our lives . . . that reaches to a different level of difficulty.

Joseph lived a life of which great novels and award-winning movies are made. He was the favorite younger son of a large family. He was honored by his earthly father and his Heavenly Father. Hated by his brothers, they faked his death and sold him into slavery. Even as a slave, he distinguished himself as a leader, rising to a place of prominence and then being falsely accused of sexual misconduct. He was given insight from God, rose to another position of power and became one of the greatest leaders of one of the powerful nations in history.

In the children's literary classic of the 1900's, "The Wonderful Wizard of Oz" by L. Frank Baum, Dorothy and Toto encounter the Wizard. After stalling to fulfill his promises, Toto pulls back a curtain and exposes the Wizard as a middle-aged man operating machinery and speaking into a microphone. Admitting to being a humbug, he insists that he is a good man but a bad wizard. Looking behind the curtain revealed the real story.

In Joseph's story, God is revealed as a "behind the scenes" Divine Chess Player moving pieces that strategically bring about His ultimate plan. As a Sovereign multi-tasker, His insight, influence and impact transcend time. His omniscient perception has been, is and will always be.

God's Good Plan. By today's standards, Joseph is a victim. The actions of his brothers and enemies are unfair and unfounded. Their deceptive reactions deliver disastrous results. Joseph's brothers devise evil against him while God designs and directs the evil for good. As Joseph places his trust in God, his perspective changes from a victim to a victor. Paul reminds us, *"And we know that God causes everything to work together for the good of those who love God and are called according to his purpose for them."* (Rom 8:28 NLT). In our lack of patience and limited perception, it's easy to lose confidence in God's plan. Our failure to trace God's moving hand requires our faith to trust His heart. Elizabeth Elliott writes, "Faith does not eliminate questions. But faith knows where to take them."[149] God always has a plan for His people.

God's Guiding Presence. God's omniscient perception is always complimented by his omnipresence . . . He is with you . . . always. George Washington writes, "Providence has at all times been my only dependence, for all other resources seemed to have failed us."[150] Moses reassures the Israelites, *"Do not be afraid or discouraged, for the Lord will personally go ahead of you. He will be with you; He will neither fail you nor abandon you."* (Deut 31:8 NLT) The Sovereign Savior has been with you in your yesterday, is with you in your today and will be with you in your tomorrow. The writer of Hebrews reminds us of God's promise, *"I will never leave you nor forsake you."* (Heb 13:5 ESV)

God's Greater Purpose. Joseph's pain, as well as his prominence are all part of God's plan for deliverance and destiny. He depends on God's grace and determines God's greater good. Joseph perceives God's broader purpose, *"He brought me to this position so I could save the lives of many people."* (Gen 50:20 NLT) Young writes, "This is how you foil the works of evil, growing in grace through the very adversity that was meant to harm you."[151] Paul tells us, *"And I am certain that God, who began the good work within you, will continue his work until it is finally finished on the day when Christ Jesus returns."* (Phil 1:6 NLT). God is working in ways that we cannot see to do things that we cannot do.

C. S. Lewis writes, "God, who foresaw your tribulation, has specially armed you to go through it, not without pain, but without stain."[152]

In our struggles and suffering, God has a good and greater purpose . . . and He guides us with His presence.

Others may devise evil . . . God has destined good. Just take a look behind the curtain.

KINGDOM THOUGHT 80: STRETCHING OUT

Above all, keep fervent in your love for one another, because love covers a multitude of sins.
1 Peter 4:8 NASB

It's been said, "The performance that really counts is your last. It's the only one most people will remember." Each and every day, we all take a step closer to our final performance. Peter reminds us, *"The end of all things is at hand . . . "* (1 Pet 4:7 ESV).

One of Peter's resolute convictions is responsive compassion. We are told to "keep fervent" or deliberate in our love toward each other. Fervent means "to be stretched out" with commitment and conviction. The disciple writes, *"You were cleansed from your sins when you obeyed the truth, so now you must show sincere (stretching) love to each other as brothers and sisters. Love each other deeply with all your heart."* (1 Pet 1:22 NLT)

Wuest writes, "The idea is the kind of a love that is extended to reach the one needing love. It is the act of one who, instead of living a self-centered life, gives of himself to others."[153]

Stretching Love Hurts. Can you remember the first time you really stretched? It hurt. Tight muscles need to be stretched in order to be flexible. Being flexible in our love is setting aside our convenience, our comfort, or our calendar. Paul writes, *"For you have been called to live in freedom, my brothers and sisters. But don't use your freedom to satisfy your sinful nature. Instead, use your freedom to serve one another in love."* (Gal 5:13 NLT)

Stretching Love Needs Help. Sometimes we need help stretching. And, the more we stretch, the easier it becomes. Paul reminds us *"Always be humble and gentle. Be patient with each other, making allowance for each other's faults because of your love. Make every effort to keep yourselves united in the Spirit, binding yourselves together with peace."* (Eph 4:2-3 NLT). We are burdened for each other; we are building each other up and we are bound together in peace.

Stretching Love Heals. Solomon reminds us, *"Hatred stirs up conflict, but love covers over all wrongs."* (Prov 10:12 NIV) Love covers insults, injuries and indiscretions . . . it doesn't collect them. The well-known "love chapter" encourages us that love, *"keeps no record of being wronged. It does not rejoice about injustice but rejoices whenever the truth wins out. Love never gives up, never loses faith, is always hopeful, and endures through every circumstance."* (1 Cor 13:5-7 NLT)

Oscar Wilde writes, "Keep love in your heart. A life without it is like a sunless garden when the flowers are dead."[154]

This life is too short to be self-centered and selfish. Decide to stretch and love . . . and let the garden God plants in your life bloom.

Kingdom Thought 81: Search and Find

That which was from the beginning, which we have heard, which we have seen with our eyes, which we have looked at and our hands have touched—this we proclaim concerning the Word of life.
1 John 1:1 NIV

A transformed life examines truth and experiences the Truth. Too often we try to rationalize the reasoning of God, instead of resting in a relationship with Him. God doesn't try to convince us . . . He changes us. A. W. Tozer writes, "We might be wise to follow the insight of the enraptured heart rather than the more cautious reasoning of the theological mind."[155]

A Life Examined. The apostle encourages us to examine Jesus, the Living Word. He tells of hearing Him, seeing Him, and even touching Him. Jesus lived among them and His followers were able to grapple with His Glory (John 1:24) . . . the Glory of God, Himself. John tells us, *"No one has ever seen God. But the unique One, who is Himself God, is near to the Father's heart. He has revealed God to us."* (John 1:18 NLT).

Walk with Him . . . talk with Him . . . rest in Him.

A Life Experienced. Once Jesus . . . His life, love and legacy have been examined; they cannot be excused . . . they must be embraced. Max Lucado writes, "Jesus tends to His people individually. He personally sees to our needs. We all receive Jesus' touch. We experience his care."[156] We are overwhelmed with opportunity by the gift of His grace. The writer to the Hebrews reminds us, *"So what makes us think we can escape if we ignore this great salvation that was first announced by the Lord Jesus himself and then delivered to us by those who heard him speak?"* (Heb 2:3 NLT).

Grab God's grace.

A Life Expressed. We must be selfless with our experience . . . we share it so others can enjoy the gift and grace of God. Eugene Peterson paraphrases John thoughts, *"We saw it, we heard it, and now we're telling you so you can experience it along with us, this experience of communion with the Father and his Son, Jesus Christ. Our motive for writing is simply this: We want you to enjoy this, too. Your joy will double our joy!"* (1 John 1:3-4 MSG).

In 1866, Arabella K. Hankey penned this second verse to the beloved hymn, "I Love To Tell The Story",

> *"I love to tell the story, more wonderful it seems,*
> *Than all the golden fancies of all our golden dreams;*
> *I love to tell the story, it did so much for me,*

And that is just the reason I tell it now to thee."

Take a moment today to tell the wonderous story of Jesus and His love.

Tim Keller writes, "All change comes from deepening your understanding of the salvation of Christ and living out the changes that understanding creates in your heart."[157]

Examine Jesus and you will find faith.

Experience Jesus and you will find hope.

Express Jesus and you will find love.

KINGDOM THOUGHT 82: TREASURE HUNTING

I want them to be encouraged and knit together by strong ties of love. I want them to have complete confidence that they understand God's mysterious plan, which is Christ Himself. In Him lie hidden all the treasures of wisdom and knowledge.
Colossians 2:2-3 NLT

Several years ago, while vacationing at the beach, we found a play area with a pirate ship clubhouse. We decided to create a treasure hunt for our grandkids. With a map, treasure chest and treasures in place, we started the hunt . . . after all, who doesn't want to be a pirate . . . who doesn't want to find buried treasure? Our grands couldn't wait to look at the map, follow the clued trail and find the treasure.

Paul reminds us that we have a rich and valued treasure in Christ. The greatest and unending wealth in wisdom and riches of knowledge is found in Him. As we walk in His presence, we find the worth of His preciousness. There are clues to the treasures He has hidden for us strategically placed along our way.

Those who seek truth and wisdom . . . living out truth and walking in wisdom . . . do so with absolute abandonment. Solomon tells us, *"Search for them as you would for silver; seek them like hidden treasures."* (Prov 2:4 NLT)

Search With Purpose. It takes commitment and conviction to be a treasure hunter. There is a hope and belief in those who possessed the treasure and most likely hid it in fear of loss or theft. The treasure found in Christ can never be lost, taken or stolen. The prophet Isaiah reminds us, *"He will be the sure foundation for your times, a rich store of salvation and wisdom and knowledge; the fear of the Lord is the key to this treasure."* (Isaiah 33:6 NIV).

Our propose is determined.

Search With Passion. Nothing detours or distracts a treasure hunter. His focus is fixed. The perspective of problems change because of the passion for the prize. Some of the trials we encounter are treasures to be embraced. These challenges of discomfort can release us from the chains of comfort. When we are loosed from our chains, we are committed to the cause. Jesus reminds His followers of the overwhelming worth of a life with God, *"The Kingdom of Heaven is like a treasure that a man discovered hidden in a field. In his excitement, he hid it again and sold everything he owned to get enough money to buy the field."* (Matt 13:44 NLT).

Our passion is deep.

Search With Promise. There is a certainty with Christ. If we look for Him, we will find Him. Solomon tells us, *"I love those who love me, and those who seek me find me."* (Proverbs 8:17 NIV). All we have to do is search, ask or inquire . . . He promises to answer in abundance. James writes, *"If you need wisdom, ask our generous God, and He will give it to you. He will not rebuke you for asking."* (Jam 1:5 NLT).

Our promise is definite.

Shauna Niequist writes, ". . . God is waiting to be found everywhere, in the darkest corners of our lives, the dead ends and bad neighborhoods we wake up in, and in the simplest, lightest, most singular and luminous moments . . . He wants to be found."[158]

Be a true Treasure hunter . . . search for Him with purpose, passion and you will receive His promise.

KINGDOM THOUGHT 83: LOOK INSIDE

Examine yourselves to see if your faith is genuine. Test yourselves. Surely you know that Jesus Christ is among you; if not, you have failed the test of genuine faith.
2 Corinthians 13:5 NLT

One of our favorite family movies that now is spanning multiple generations, is "The Lion King", both the original animation and digital re-release. At one part, Simba struggles with responsibilities that are before him . . . is he strong enough? Is he able to be all that is required of him? Can he do what he is tasked to do? Mufasa's image comes to Simba and says, "Look inside yourself, you are more than what you have become."

At different times in our lives, we may experience comfort and ease or chaos and economic struggle. In each of these times, at every turn and at every intersection of doubt and destiny, we need to look inside to see what God is doing and how He is working in our hearts.

We are challenged to examine ourselves . . . or look inside . . . on a regular basis. Eugene Peterson in his paraphrased work, The Message, reminds us of Paul's thoughts, *"Make a careful exploration of who you are and the work you have been given, and then sink yourself into that. Don't be impressed with yourself. Don't compare yourself with others."* (Gal 6:4 MSG)

As we look inside, we are reminded that as God touches us, we touch others. As we look in, we begin living out. Here are some thoughts on looking inside and living outside . . .

We Bless Others Because We Have Been Blessed. In his letter to the Ephesians, Paul reminds us that we have been blessed with every spiritual blessing in Christ Jesus (Eph 1:3). When we look inside at all the ways God has blessed us, we are able to be a blessing to others. Wise King Solomon reminds us, *"Whoever brings blessing will be enriched, and one who waters will himself be watered."* (Proverbs 11:25)

We Love Others Because We Have Been Loved. Jesus deliverers and demonstrates love since He is love. We are told that we love, only because we have been first loved by God. (1 John 4:19) As we walk in this life, opportunities come before us each and every day to show love and to share the love of God. The disciple John reminds us that there is no fear in love (1 John 4:18). If fear is present, love is absent. And, if love is experienced, fear has exited. Our healing can be another's hope. Steve Maraboli writes, "A kind gesture can reach a wound that only compassion can heal."[159]

We Give Because We Have Been Given. John reminds us, *"If someone has enough money to live well and sees a brother or sister in need but shows no compassion—how can God's love be in that person? Dear children, let's not merely say that we love each other; let us show the truth by our actions."* (I John 3:17-18 NLT) We give . . . following the example of God. The beloved disciples writes, *"This is how much God loved the world: He gave his Son, his one and only Son. And this is why: so that no one need be destroyed; by believing in him, anyone can have a whole and lasting life."* (John 3:16 MSG) He loves . . . He gives! We love . . . we give. If we are not giving, we are not loving.

We Serve Because We Have Been Served. The heart of a believer, of a Christ-follower is seen in one who serves. Jesus says, *"For even the Son of Man came not to be served but to serve others and to give his life as a ransom for many."* (Mark 10:45 NLT). He did not come to be served . . . but to serve . . . and He has given us that example to follow.

Inspirational writer and speaker, Israelmore Ayivor writes, "The only way to make a damaged machine work again is to break it down, work on its inner system and fix it again. Screw out the bolts of your life, examine and work on yourself, fix your life again and get going."[160]

Peterson gives some insight, *"Test yourselves to make sure you are solid in the faith. Don't drift along taking everything for granted. Give yourselves regular checkups. You need firsthand evidence, not mere hearsay, that Jesus Christ is in you. Test it out."* (2 Cor 13:5 MSG)

Give yourself a checkup. Take a look on the inside . . . Blessings . . . Loving . . . Giving . . . Serving. Through Christ, you are more than what you have become . . . test it out.

KINGDOM THOUGHT 84: CONVICTION

A new commandment I give to you, that you love one another: just as I have loved you, you also are to love one another. By this all people will know that you are my disciples, if you have love for one another.
John 13:34-35 ESV

Jesus introduces a radical instruction . . . a new truth that requires new thinking.

Love is no longer a comfortable convenience . . . it is a compassionate conviction.

Pamela Rose Williams writes, "Sometimes it's difficult to love someone. It's easy to love the lovely people; but what about those unlovely people that we come in contact with sometimes on a daily basis?" [161]

As disciples of Christ, our compassion becomes our calling card. The expression of our love is the evidence of our heart.

A New Instruction. The rules of religion often replace the priority for relationships within the redeemed. Too many times, we expect right actions before we extend righteous affection. Jesus reduces all of the commandments to two. He reminds us, *"'And you shall love the Lord your God with all your heart and with all your soul and with all your mind and with all your strength.' The second is this: 'You shall love your neighbor as yourself.' There is no other commandment greater than these."* (Mark 12:30-31 ESV) God's love is based on Who He is, not on what we do. This is revolutionary in God's Church.

A New Intention. Barbara De Angelis reminds us, "You never lose by loving. You always lose by holding back."[162] Just as we have received God's love, we return it to others. Our love for others is comprehensive and completely modeled after Christ's love for us. We are a funnel through which His compassion flows. The more we are intimate in our longing for Him, the more we are intentional with our love to others. John tells us what this intentional love looks like. He writes, *"By this we know love, that He laid down his life for us, and we ought to lay down our lives for the brothers. But if anyone has the world's goods and sees his brother in need, yet closes his heart against him, how does God's love abide in him? Little children, let us not love in word or talk but in deed and in truth."* (1 John 3:16-18 ESV) We give out of the grace we have received. We live out the love that God lavishes on us.

A New Identifier. The Nike swoosh. Ralph Lauren's polo rider. McDonald's golden arches. Brand marketing creates a symbol that causes immediate recognition of a product, concept or service. These symbols are often known as logos. Our love becomes our logo. When we love each other . . . with selflessness, sacrifice and service . . . we brand ourselves as being followers of Christ. The psalmist reminds us of the depth and devotion of God's love, *"The LORD is compassionate and merciful, slow to get angry and filled with unfailing love."* (Ps 103:8 NLT). It's a love that's decisive and not divisive. It's a love that is constructive, not destructive. It's a love that builds up, not tears down.

Jimmy Larche writes, "The true mark of Christ followers is that they have love for one another. This is what comes to define us. When we don't follow Christ in his love for people, we end up reducing Christianity to something else – typically a cheap substitute disguised as religious devotion."[163]

God has shown us love and we share His love with others. Oscar Wilde pens this thought, "Keep love in your heart. A life without it is like a sunless garden when the flowers are dead. The consciousness of loving and being loved brings a warmth and richness to life that nothing else can bring."[164]

It's great instruction with grace-filled intentions and a God identifier . . . receive His love and give it away.

KINGDOM THOUGHT 85: WHERE I'M GOING

For everything comes from Him and exists by His power and is intended for His glory. All glory to Him forever! Amen.
Romans 11:36 NLT

There's an old Irish blessing that reads, "May you have the hindsight to know where you've been, the foresight to know where you are going, and the insight to know when you have gone too far."

If you know where you've come from and where you want to go . . . you can figure out where you are. It's identifying the starting point and investing in the satisfying place.

Paul reminds the Christ-followers in Rome that their greatest satisfaction is in God, "I plead with you to give your bodies to God because of all He has done for you. Let them be a living and holy sacrifice — the kind He will find acceptable. This is truly the way to worship Him." (Rom 12:1 NLT) Honoring God results in humbling ourselves and helping others.

It's All From Him. Our God has given us a beginning. The apostle reminds us, *"Christ is the visible image of the invisible God . . . for through Him God created everything in the heavenly realms and on earth. He made the things we can see and the things we can't see . . . everything was created through Him and for Him."* (Col 1:15-16 NLT). We are not a mistake or an error . . . we are His masterpiece and His expression. Each day is a gift of creation . . . they are fresh and full of opportunity. James tells us, *"Whatever is good and perfect is a gift coming down to us from God our Father, who created all the lights in the heavens. He never changes or casts a shifting shadow."* (Jam 1:17 NLT)

It's All By Him. Our God has given us a because. One insurance company reminds us that we "are in safe hands" and can find security in their services. An older spiritual song says, "He's got the whole world in His hands." Paul encourages us that God's hands are safe and strong, *"He existed before anything else, and He holds all creation together."* (Col 1:17 NLT) Jesus is the meaning for every moment. He reminds us that coincidences are really the coordinated efforts of His hand.

It's All For Him. Our God has given us a blessing. In, by and for His glory . . . He gives us purpose, power and possibility. All that we do is intended for His glory . . . not our own. Jude provides powerful closing comments in his epistle, *"And now to Him who can keep you on your feet, standing tall in his bright presence, fresh and celebrating—to our one God, our only Savior, through Jesus Christ, our Master, be glory, majesty, strength, and rule before all time, and now,* *and to the end of all time. Amen."* (Jude 1:24-25 MSG)

Matthew Henry writes, "Paul knew the mysteries of the kingdom of God as well as ever any man; yet he confesses himself at a loss; and despairing to find the bottom, he humbly sits down at the brink, and adores the depth."

In our desperation, we stop . . . sit . . . and surrender to His deity.

He is your beginning. He is your because. He is your blessing.

Express your gratitude . . . give Him the glory. This, my friend is where we are going.

KINGDOM THOUGHT 86: A DAD'S LOVE

So he returned home to his father. And while he was still a long way off, his father saw him coming. Filled with love and compassion, he ran to his son, embraced him, and kissed him.
Luke 15:20 NLT

Being a dad is the hardest thing I've ever done.

I've been at this "father" thing for almost 40 years. Once I think I have a handle on it, I find that I've lost my grip. When I think I have arrived, I realize I'm still on a journey. Pope John XXIII says, "It is easier for a father to have children than for children to have a real father."[165]

Jesus' influence and instruction created great interest to those who were not on the "inside". Luke tells us, *"Tax collectors and other notorious sinners often came to listen to Jesus teach."* (Luke 15:1 NLT). He was different, He was dynamic, and He was deliberate. He "rattled some cages" because His love was reaching, redeeming and restorative.

This type of compassion causes controversy. The Scripture reads, "This made the Pharisees and teachers of religious law complain that He was associating with such sinful people—even eating with them!" (vs 2)

To illustrate the heart of God, Jesus tells three stories. The last parable illustrates a father's passion and priority . . . it's the account of The Prodigal Son. There are so many layers of lessons . . . yet, the attitude and action of the father provides a priority of and pathway to parenting.

He Longs. In this story, the prodigal has serious issues. His entitlement leads to his emptiness. He sets aside the learning from his childhood and trades them for a lusty life. Instead of embracing wisdom, he excessively wastes all he has. He screws up and messes up. He has it all and loses it all. Yet, through humility, he turns his heart around. We often focus on the son's "giving in", but the bigger story is his dad's refusal to "give up". I'm going to presume that the prodigal's father made it a habit to hope for his son's return. He was anticipating, waiting and longing. Compassionate grace takes the place of condemning guilt. The prophet Isaiah writes, *"Yet the Lord longs to be gracious to you; therefore, He will rise up to show you compassion."* (Isaiah 30:18 NIV).

He Looks. *"And while he was still a long way off, his father saw him coming."* (Luke 15:20 NLT). I've often wondered how many days this dad was looking "a long way off"? I would surmise that searching the horizon each morning and each evening was part of his routine. His father didn't know the condition of his son's heart, yet he was still longing and looking for him. Brown writes, "Oh yes, when but the face is turned homeward, though as yet far, far away, our Father recognizes His own child in us, and bounds to meet us—not saying, 'Let him come to Me and sue for pardon first', but Himself taking the first step."[166] When a child is helpless and in destitute despair, a merciful father is scanning the horizon with hope of healing.

He Loves. He longs for his son's return. He looks for his son's return. And, he loves his son when he returns. There is not an accounting of wrongs. There is not a time of "I told you so". Luke reminds us, *"Filled with love and compassion, he ran to his son, embraced him, and kissed him."* (Luke 15:20 NLT). The father's acceptance is evident in his affection . . . he runs, he embraces, and he kisses him. When the son takes the first step, his father runs the rest of the way. In his work, The Message, Peterson gives insight into Paul's writings, *"It's a wonder God didn't lose his temper and do away with the whole lot of us. Instead, immense in mercy and with an incredible love, He embraced us. He took our sin-dead lives and made us alive in Christ. He did all this on His own, with no help from us!"* (Eph 2:4-5 MSG)

John Ciardi writes, "Every parent is at some time the father of the unreturned prodigal, with nothing to do but keep his house open to hope."[167]

A father's love . . . he longs, he looks, and he loves. As a dad, never gives up . . . even if they've gone away.

For some, this may be one of the hardest things you've ever done . . . but . . . it will be the best thing you will ever do.

KINGDOM THOUGHT 87: BUILDING UP

We should help others do what is right and build them up in the Lord.
Romans 15:2 NLT

There is an undefinable and undeniable strength that comes from following Christ. This strength instills confidence, courage and conviction. It allows us to attempt great things for Him as well as rest in His grace. Paul reminds Timothy that, *"God has not given us a spirit of fear and timidity, but of power, love, and self-discipline."* (2 Tim 1:7 NLT)

Some use their power and strength for control and condemnation. This only creates insecurity, insensitivity and indifference. Strength from God is characterized with devotion for others and discipline of self. It's not about what we can be but what we can do for others. Eugene Peterson, in The Message reminds us, *"Strength is for service, not status".* (Rom 15:2)

In Paul's writings, the early believers in Rome are discovering and defining an understanding of what it means to be a strong follower of Christ. Some experience a freedom of grace, while others exercise a formation of guidelines. Some are strong in their faith, while others struggle as they grow. It is not about proving who is right or pleasing self . . . it was about peacefully and practically serving others. Paul writes, *"We who are strong must be considerate of those who are sensitive about things like this. We must not just please ourselves."* (Romans 15:1 NLT). This juxtaposition requires delicate decisions and peaceful practices.

Empathetic Willingness. Paul tells us, *"we should help others do what is right"*. Some feel this is done by proclamation . . . telling others what to do. The apostle motivates us to participation . . . helping others with what needs to be done. Often, we give strength to those who are struggling or suffering. Dietrich Bonhoeffer writes, "We must learn to regard people less in the light of what they do or omit to do, and more in the light of what they suffer."[168] Empathy requires a willing effort to engage. The writer of Hebrews encourages us, *"Let us think of ways to motivate one another to acts of love and good works."* (Heb 10:24 NLT)

Encouraging Words. Our words need to be constructive, not condemning. Discouraging words erect a wall, while encouraging words build a bridge. Solomon reminds us, *"Worry weighs a person down; an encouraging word cheers a person up."* (Prov 12:25 NLT). Our source of encouragement comes from our strength in our Savior. Isaiah writes, *"The Sovereign LORD has given me his words of wisdom, so that I know how to comfort the weary."* (Is 50:4 NLT)

Exercising Walk. I'm a fan of fitness, to some degree. I'm also a fan of friendship. Helen Keller writes, "Walking with a friend in the dark is better than walking alone in the light."[169] Some of our most significant journeys are when we accompany someone walking through life's valleys. It not only becomes a blessing to them, but a process of building up. The disciple whom Jesus loved reminds us, *"But if we walk in the light, as He is in the light, we have fellowship with one another, and the blood of Jesus, His Son, purifies us from all sin."* (1 John 1:7 NIV) Willingness and words, at times are not enough . . . walking with someone may be the only way to strengthen their heart. Matthew Henry writes, "It's not talking but walking that will bring us to heaven."[170]

Leo Buscaglia pens these thoughts, "Too often we underestimate the power of a touch, a smile, a kind word, a listening ear, an honest compliment, or the smallest act of caring, all of which have the potential to turn a life around."[171]

May our strength in Christ be evidenced by our service to others.

May our confidence in Him be seen in our compassion.

May our boldness be characterized by our blessing of others.

Kingdom Thought 88: Fallen & Can't Get Up

Now all glory to God, Who is able to keep you from falling away and will bring you with great joy into His glorious presence without a single fault.
Jude 1:24 NLT

I really don't like having a falling dream. It's been awhile . . . but the resulting anxiety and fear is vivid. Studies tells us that every person has at least five falling dreams in their lifetime. Dream analyzers write, "When we fall in our dreams it really means we have lost control with some sort of situation in our life. Falling in your dream is a way our unconscious communicates with our conscious to let us know that something needs to be fixed right away."[172]

Left to our own strength and strategies, we are all susceptible to slipping. In many situations, we have already lost control. Often, there are so many areas that need to be fixed, that we can give into failure. Trying to stand our own two feet in a *"slimy pit, in the mud and mire"* (Ps 40:2) is an unlikely, if not impossible task.

Peterson, in The Message, relates Jude's thoughts that Jesus *"can keep you on your feet, standing tall in His bright presence, fresh and celebrating"*. (Jude 1:24 MSG). It begins with surrendering to His strength, strategies and sovereign control.

He Keeps Us From Falling. God's promise to keep us from falling proposes that we have a propensity to fall. We need God. Our dependence on self can lead to our destruction of self. Jesus is the only one who can give us new power, new perspective and new potential. David reminds us, *"He lifted me out of the pit of despair, out of the mud and the mire. He set my feet on solid ground and steadied me as I walked along."* (Psalms 40:2 NLT). He wants to and will keep us from falling.

He Brings Us Joyfully Into His Presence. We've gone to a lot of weddings in our lifetime. Everyone has their "favorite" part of the ceremony. Personally, mine is when the couple is presented for the first time as husband and wife. At that moment, vows and rings have been exchanged, the groom has kissed the bride, the ceremony is almost completed, and the pressure is gone . . . and, with great excitement and joy, a new "Mr. and Mrs." is presented. Christ does the same with us. He presents us as His new bride . . . with immeasurable joy, He announces that we are His . . . accepted, approved and adored. Isaiah writes, *"Just as a young man commits himself to his bride. Then God will rejoice over you* *as a bridegroom rejoices over his bride."* (Is 62:5 NLT) We can't bring ourselves into His presence . . . God brings us. It's not anything that we do . . . it's only what He does.

He Remembers No Fault. God doesn't keep a legal pad of all our sins. He has erased every single one of them and washed them clean with the cleansing blood of Jesus. Our mistakes have been covered in mercy. Our gross sins have been showered with grace. Our fears and failures have been traded because of faith. David reminds us, *"As far as the east is from the west, so far does He remove our transgressions from us."* (Ps 103:12 ESV). When God looks at you, He doesn't say, "not again" . . . He says, "never again". Because of Jesus, we are faultless and free.

Feel like you're slipping . . . sinking . . . stumbling? Our God will keep you from falling with His mighty hand. He confidently and joyfully welcomes you into His comforting arms. And, no matter what you've done . . . how much you have failed . . . or how disappointing you may have been . . . there is no fault in Him or with Him.

Jesus "can keep you on your feet, standing tall in His bright presence, fresh and celebrating".

KINGDOM THOUGHT 89: DOING LOVE

Dear children, let's not merely say that we love each other; let us show the truth by our actions.
1 John 3:18 NLT

It's been said, "Love is not a noun that needs to be defined, but a verb that needs to be demonstrated."[173]

The validity of our love is verified by our walk, not our words.

In his writings to 1st century Christ followers, John communicates a clarifying conviction of compassion. He illustrates Jesus' impactful instruction, *"Your love for one another will prove to the world that you are my disciples."* (Jn 13:35 NLT)

The proof is not so much in the "pudding", as in the practice.

Love Puts In. Love is an investment in others that provides an immeasurable return. It's living by love . . . it's giving in grace. The disciple, John tells us, *"Beloved, if God so loved us, we also ought to love one another."* (1 Jn 4:11 ESV). Our compassion for others creates a contributing cause. Mitch Albom writes, "The way you get meaning into your life is to devote yourself to loving others, devote yourself to your community around you, and devote yourself to creating something that gives you purpose and meaning."[174]

Love Puts Up. Love is an adoring acceptance and a tender tolerance. Paul reminds us, *"Always be humble and gentle. Be patient with each other, making allowance for each other's faults because of your love."* (Eph 4:2 NLT). Love does not condemn, it covers. Solomon writes, *"Hatred stirs up strife, but love covers all offenses."* (Prov 10:12 ESV).

Love Puts Out. This phrase will undoubtedly raise some eyebrows. The measure by which we receive God's love from others is minimal compared to our response of God's love to others. Expressing His compassion is a walking, willing and worshiping experience. John establishes the litmus test of love. He writes, *"We know what real love is because Jesus gave up his life for us. So, we also ought to give up our lives for our brothers and sisters. If someone has enough money to live well and sees a brother or sister in need but shows no compassion—how can God's love be in that person?"* (1 Jn 3:16-17 NLT). Sharing God's love unshackles us to serve others. Paul writes, *"For you have been called to live in freedom, my brothers and sisters. But don't use your freedom to satisfy your sinful nature. Instead, use your freedom to serve one another in love."* (Gal 5:13 NLT)

Unselfish love leads to an undeniable legacy. In a challenge to next-generation leaders, Kay Warren says, "The depth to which we can give and receive compassion is the benchmark by which we measure the success of our lives."[175]

Let's not just define love . . . let's allow it to redefine us.

KINGDOM THOUGHT 90: FAILED AGAIN

Brothers and sisters, I do not consider myself yet to have taken hold of it. But one thing I do: forgetting what is behind and straining toward what is ahead, I press on toward the goal to win the prize for which God has called me heavenward in Christ Jesus.
Philippians 3:13-14 NIV

I can't tell you how many times I've failed.

Failing is part of a normal, healthy and growing life. How many times does a child fail at walking before they're running through a home? How many drivers on the road failed their first driving test? How many great recipes originate as culinary disasters?

It's tough to get back up after we've been knocked down. . . . but we do get back up. Our failings deepen our faith, our errors educate us and our rejections lead to resilience. Teddy Roosevelt says, "The only man who never makes a mistake is the man who never does anything."[176]

The words of the apostle Paul are encouraging. This life of falling, falling and faltering must include forgetting what is behind and straining, stretching and striving for what lies ahead.

When we begin to move courageously, we encounter combative resistance. Opportunity will always bring opposition . . . and often opposition will create obstacles. The Deceiver uses these obstacles or failings as a passive paralyzer that strike at the core of our spiritual nervous system. He tries to stop us . . . dead in our tracks.

Keathley writes, "A study of Bible characters reveals that most of those who made history were men who failed at some point, and some of them drastically, but who refused to continue lying in the dust."[177]

Abraham, Moses, Elijah, David, and Peter are just a few who can list failing in their resume. Their failures were significant and staggering. But, each rejected the notion that failing made them a failure. They repented, recovered and rebounded . . . yes . . . they bounced back. These faulty and flawed men grew from experience and by faith, embraced a renewed mission for God.

Grieving In Our Failure. Confession is good for the soul. There is a time to grieve for failings. David reminds us, *"The sacrifice you desire is a broken spirit. You will not reject a broken and repentant heart, O God."* (Ps 51:17 NLT) Moving forward begins with forgiveness. It becomes a comforting reality that God knows our faults and failings . . . and unreservedly forgives. Often a listening ear and an loving word can help. James encourages us to *"confess your sins to each other* *and pray for each other so that you may be healed."* (Jam 5:16 NLT)

Growing In Our Failure. Erwin Lutzer reminds us that "failure is the back door to success."[178] Growth from our failings gives a more solid foundation . . . we know what not to do again. Keathley writes, "Sometimes God must engineer failure in us before He can bring about success with us. Our failures are often rungs on the ladder of growth—if we will learn from our mistakes rather than grovel in the dirt."[179] As Paul reminds us, we must "press on". Jesus encourages Simon Peter, *"Simon, stay on your toes. Satan has tried his best to separate all of you from me, like chaff from wheat. Simon, I've prayed for you in particular that you not give in or give out. When you have come through the time of testing, turn to your companions and give them a fresh start."* (Luke 22:31-32 MSG). The historian James Anthony Froude writes, "The worth of a man must be measured by his life, not by his failure under a singular and peculiar trial."[180] We grieve and we grow.

Grace In Our Failure. The apostle tells us, *"where sin increased, grace increased all the more."* (Rom 5:20 NIV). Failure and repentance usher in a more vivid understanding of the grace of God in each of us. Paul finds a solution in his struggles. He writes, *"Each time God said, 'My grace is all you need. My power works best in weakness.' So now I am glad to boast about my weaknesses, so that the power of Christ can work through me. That's why I take pleasure in my weaknesses, and in the insults, hardships, persecutions, and troubles that I suffer for Christ. For when I am weak, then I am strong."* (2 Cor 12:9-10 NLT) We grieve, we grow, and we receive God's grace.

At the age of 67 Thomas Edison lost most of his life's work in a tragic fire. The morning following the fire Edison looked at the ruins and said, "There is great value in disaster. All our mistakes are burned up. Thank God we can start anew."[181] Three weeks later, he invented the phonograph.

If you've been knocked down, get back up. If fear and failing have paralyzed you, just move a little bit . . . a successful journey begins with the first step. Be defined by your faith, not your failures.

Our God gives grace for this race. Press on.

KINGDOM THOUGHT 91: BREAK THE MOLD

The LORD says, "I will guide you along the best pathway for your life. I will advise you and watch over you."
Psalms 32:8 NLT

I'm more of a "go for it" guy instead of a "guide me" guy.

I recall whitewater rafting in Colorado. Our guide was very specific in how we should approach certain rapids, currents and eddies. He cautioned us to walk with him down to "putting-in" at just the right spot. He also stressed the importance of working with him, trusting him and depending on his expertise. And, he was emphatic about waiting for his instructions. He knew the river . . . and, we didn't. I really got wet that day . . . more so than needed.

God draws on His care and compassion to guide us each and every day. He knows our yesterday, today and our tomorrow . . . and, He wants to guide us in His grace.

Walk With Him. Each day, God waits for us to walk with Him . . . to invite Him into our schedule, to listen to His insight and to trust His guiding. The prophet Isaiah tells the weary and wayward nation of Israel of God's willingness to walk with them. He writes, *"And your ears shall hear a word behind you, saying, 'This is the way, walk in it,' when you turn to the right or when you turn to the left."* (Is 30:21 ESV) We can walk our own path in our own power and with our own perceptions . . . or we can purposely walk in God's path. Young gives insight in our walking with God, "One way is to moan and groan, stumbling along with shuffling feet. This will get you to the end of the day eventually, but there is a better way. You can choose to walk with [God] along the path of peace, leaning on [Him] as much as you need. There will still be difficulties along the way, but you can face them confidently in [His] strength."

Work With Him. This excursion with God requires an effort. Paul reminds the Christ followers in Philippi, *"work out your own salvation with fear and trembling, for it is God who works in you, both to will and to work for His good pleasure."* (Phil 2:12-13 ESV) A. A. Conrad writes of God, "He sees the perils that are in our path that we cannot see. He speaks to us in mercy and grace and He builds us up to meet the dangers and be prepared to receive the things we could not wisely use today."[182] We do the hard work of surrendering and He does the holy work of sanctifying. Don't forget . . . it's work and it's worth it.

Wait On Him. Many of us hate giving up control and patiently waiting for God to do something. It may be in our finances, friendships or your future . . . we just want Him to work . . . and to do it now! Henri Nouwen reminds us, "One of the most arduous spiritual tasks is that of giving up control and allowing the Spirit of God to lead our lives."[183] Peterson, in The Message, reminds of Isaiah's insight, *"GOD doesn't come and go. God lasts."* (Is 40:28 MSG). He writes, *"But those who wait upon GOD get fresh strength. They spread their wings and soar like eagles, They run and don't get tired, they walk and don't lag behind."* (Is 40:31 MSG). Worn out . . . wait on Him. Weary . . . wait on Him. Weak . . . wait on Him.

Skip Moen writes, "God does not come to us in nicely defined, rationally explained, thought categories. God does not fit Himself into our theological textbooks. The Hebrew God breaks all the rules. He is near, yet transcendent; clothed in human form, yet holy; more terrifying than can be imagined, yet compassionate; invisible, yet revealed; judging, yet merciful; sovereign, yet humble. No matter where you look, God breaks the molds."[184]

Walk with Him. Allow Him to do His great work. And, wait for His timing.

Today, let God break the mold.

Kingdom Thought 92: Peacemaker

May God, who gives this patience and encouragement, help you live in complete harmony with each other, as is fitting for followers of Christ Jesus.
Romans 15:5 NLT

It's easier for me to be a "pot-stirrer" instead of a "peacemaker".

Although God longs for us to live in peace and harmony, we tend to live in conflict and chaos. Some followers of Jesus are more apt to shoot those who are wounded instead of performing triage, much less help with the healing process.

And, there are some who see scars . . . whether they be physical, emotional, social or spiritual . . . as a reminder of shortcomings or sin instead of survival and sanctification.

The challenge comes with those who promote repentance yet have a problem with restoration.

As the Apostle Paul writes, the 1st century church in Rome is wrestling with living in peace, living in harmony and living in acceptance. There is a struggle between those who experience freedom in Christ and with those who embrace security in stringent and strict life choices. Paul teaches an acceptance of both . . . walking in unity and practicing grace . . . as well as, patience and encouragement through selflessness.

Our Example. Jesus provides a role model of thinking more of others and less of self. Paul reminds us, *"For even Christ didn't live to please himself."* (Rom 15:3 NLT). When we serve others, we surrender all of our wants and needs to Jesus. Paul writes to the believers in Philippi, *"Don't be selfish; don't try to impress others. Be humble, thinking of others as better than yourselves. Don't look out only for your own interests, but take an interest in others, too. You must have the same attitude that Christ Jesus had."* (Phil 2:3-5 NLT). Self-promotion is a steppingstone to sinful pride. It's all about God's Kingdom, not our own.

Our Encouragement. Most people are not prone to patience or experts at encouragement. Through God's written and living word, we have the hope and help to live in grace and giving. Paul writes, *"Such things were written in the Scriptures long ago to teach us. And the Scriptures give us hope and encouragement as we wait patiently for God's promises to be fulfilled."* (Rom 15:4 NLT). The result of our hope for tomorrow is harmony today. Practicing patience and peace is the proper protocol for those who have been redeemed, renewed and restored. Solomon reminds us, *"Worry weighs a person down; an encouraging word cheers a person up."* (Prov 12:25 NLT)

Our Expectation. There are positive results from living in harmony and peace. The greatest are hallelujahs and praise. The apostle encourages the Christ followers in Rome, *"May God . . . help you live in complete harmony with each other, as is fitting for followers of Christ Jesus. Then all of you can join together with one voice, giving praise and glory to God, the Father of our Lord Jesus Christ."* (Rom 15:5-6 NLT). We join with other sinners saved by grace, with other wounded soldiers who have been healed, with the broken who have been mended, with set free captives, with fallen who have been lifted, with rejected who have been accepted . . . and with one voice and one heart . . . give praise to the Prince of Peace and exaltation to the Everlasting Encourager.

Paul gives a closing summary, "Therefore, accept each other just as Christ has accepted you so that God will be given glory." (Rom 15:7 NLT)

Jessy and Bryan Matteo write, "Even the smallest act of caring for another person is like a drop of water . . . it will make ripples throughout the entire pond."[185]

We give grace and He gets the glory.

Be a peacemaker and make some ripples in the pond.

KINGDOM THOUGHT 93: WISE WORDS

Live wisely among those who are not believers, and make the most of every opportunity. Let your conversation be gracious and attractive so that you will have the right response for everyone.
Colossians 4:5-6 NLT

Living wisely, with Kingdom impact and influence is one of our great opportunities. It's exercising God's principles into our daily processes. Wise living becomes the track on which our testimony runs. It leads others to a divine destination. Paul is one of the many Biblical authors who remind us that our speech and conversation can derail, detour or destroy our opportunity to have Kingdom introductions and influence.

Too often, I'm guilty of it . . . Sarcasm. Harsh words. Cutting remarks. Unkind responses. Demeaning comments. Derogatory slurs. Backhanded shots. Double-meaning gab. Passive aggressive puns.

These choice words don't build up, rather they tear down. These cosmetic comments make us look better than we are while making others look worse than they are. These words are not kind.

Words that are gracious and attractive provide us the greatest opportunity for Kingdom impact.

Words That Are Appropriate. Paul cautions the Christ-followers in Ephesus, "Let no corrupting talk come out of your mouths, but only such as is good for building up, as fits the occasion, that it may give grace to those who hear." (Eph 4:29 ESV). The right words for the right situation are redemptive and restoring. At times our words need to be firm and forceful, yet still fair. Solomon gives wise instruction, *"A gentle answer turns away wrath, but a harsh word stirs up anger."* (Prov 15:1 NIV)

Words That Are Appealing. Gracious conversation is complimented with grace. Matthew Henry writes, *"Though it be not always of grace, it must always be with grace."* Our words are benefiting, not burdensome. Solomon reminds us, *"The hearts of the wise make their mouths prudent, and their lips promote instruction. Gracious words are a honeycomb, sweet to the soul and healing to the bones."* (Prov 16:23-24 NIV). Encouraging words embrace the soul.

Words That Are Attractive. Peter writes, "But in your hearts revere Christ as Lord. Always be prepared to give an answer to everyone who asks you to give the reason for the hope that you have. But do this with gentleness and respect," (1 Pet 3:15 NIV). Our conversation compliments our convictions. Solomon tells us that our healing and helping words give hope. He writes, "The soothing tongue is a tree of life, but a perverse tongue crushes the spirit." (Prov 15:4 NIV)

Poets know the power of words. Songwriters understand their significance. Authors influence imagination with their imagery. Words have power . . . to heal or to hurt . . . to develop or destroy . . . to release or restrain.

Mother Teresa says, "Kind words can be short and easy to speak, but their echoes are truly endless."[186]

So, today will I speak . . .

Words that heal or words that hurt.

Words that build up or words that tear down.

Words that open or words that close.

Words that encourage or words that discourage.

Words that promote faith or words that produce fear.

Words that invite or words that isolate.

Words of inclusion or words of exclusion.

Words of peace or words of war.

Words of confirmation or words of condemnation.

Words of hope or words of despair.

Words that are just right or words that are just wrong.

Words of instruction or words of incompetence.

Words that are just enough or words that are more than needed.

Words that are life-giving or words that are life-taking.

Make the most of every opportunity . . . speak encouraging words that will influence, inspire and impact . . . and, the echoes of your words will be truly endless.

KINGDOM THOUGHT 94: GOD'S SCHEDULE

The LORD directs the steps of the godly. He delights in every detail of their lives.
Psalms 37:23 NLT

Providence. Sovereignty. Predestination. It's challenging to be comfortable with, much less comprehend the broad scope of these words.

I recently had one of those days that wasn't planned, scheduled or organized the way I had thought . . . but, there's no doubt God had His fingerprints all over it. Too often, we organize our days down to the minute. We commit our days to God, even asking Him to bless us and guide us. Yet, when His sovereign hand redirects our day, we become frantic and fearful. We often shift into "survival" mode thinking our skills and smarts will get us through our disrupted schedule.

God can be trusted as the perfect planner. He knows every detail. He is the Sovereign multi-tasker, organizing tomorrow's opportunities through today's obstacles. He is involved in our past, impacting our present and influencing our future. He simply requires that our faith in Him replace our fears of the day.

I Can Be Confident. We can walk each day with complete confidence. Paul reminds us, *"Being confident of this very thing, that he which hath begun a good work in you will perform it until the day of Jesus Christ."* (Phil 1:6 KJV). We are able to live in the continuous circle of God's glory and our good. I am confident in His commitment and character.

I can be secure in His sovereignty.

He Is In Control. The first century believers in Rome had the assurance of God's control. Paul encourages them, *"And we know that God causes everything to work together for the good of those who love God and are called according to his purpose for them."* (Rom 8:28 NLT) S. Micheal Houdmann writes, "Nothing is random or comes by chance, especially not in the lives of believers. He 'purposed' it."[187] Isaiah reminds us, *"I make known the end from the beginning, from ancient times, what is still to come. I say: My purpose will stand, and I will do all that I please"* (Is 46:10 ESV)

I can have confidence in His control.

He Is Compassionate. Paul asks and answers *"Can anything ever separate us from Christ's love? Does it mean He no longer loves us if we have trouble or calamity, or are persecuted, or hungry, or destitute, or in danger, or threatened with death? No, despite all these things, overwhelming victory is ours through Christ, who loved us."* (Rom 8:35, 37 NLT) Even when we feel like we're disconnected from God, our faith keeps us in touch with Him. Chip Ingram encourages us, "Even if your emotional connection with Him isn't always there, God is still near."[188] The prophet Zephaniah writes, *"The Lord your God is with you. He's mighty to deliver. He takes great delight in you. He will quiet you with His love. He rejoices over you with singing."* (Zep 3:17 ESV)

I can have comfort in His compassion.

Be assured that God not only directs your path . . . He also delights in every detail.

In 1993, Twila Paris recorded an impacting song about God. The lyrics read:

> *This is not time for fear,*
> *This is the time for faith and determination.*
> *Don't lose the vision here carried away by the motion,*
> *Hold on to all that you hide in your heart.*
> *There is one thing that has always been true,*
> *He holds the world together.*
> *God is in control.*
> *We believe that His children will not be forsaken.*
> *God is in control.*
> *We will choose to remember and never be shaken.*
> *There is no power above or beside Him, we know,*
> *Oh, God is in control, oh God is in control.*
> *He has never let you down.*
> *Why start to worry now?*
> *He is still the Lord of all we see,*
> *And He is still the loving Father,*
> *Watching over you and me.*
> *God is in control.*

Let God's schedule determine your day . . . even down to the smallest detail.

KINGDOM THOUGHT 95: HERE'S WHAT I THINK

This foolish plan of God is wiser than the wisest of human plans, and God's weakness is stronger than the greatest of human strength.
1 Corinthians 1:25 NLT

I've often wondered why God doesn't ask for my advice.

Don't I see things that the omnipresent God can't see? Don't I know things that the omniscient God doesn't know? I think I have some really good ideas (not really).

I think I know a great deal, when in reality, I know very little. The pretense of my insight and wisdom promotes my insignificance and waning. Pride effects perception. Saint Augustine reminds us, "We were ensnared by the wisdom of the serpent; we are set free by the foolishness of God."

God loves us. Yet, His passion does not permit our prominence. Alistair Begg writes, "God's concern is for His name, His glory, His people, His unfolding eternal purpose and for His Kingdom."[189] It's all about Him.

So, I've been asking . . . what does God want from me?

God Wants My Heart More Than My Help. God appreciates our affection for Him over our assistance to Him. Solomon reminds us, *"O my son, give me your heart. May your eyes take delight in following my ways."* (Prov 23:26 NLT). When we follow God's ways, we find our work.

God Wants My Surrender More Than My Strengths. If God has made me the way I am, why doesn't He use my strengths, abilities, aptitudes? I'm still learning . . . God wants us to "give over" control, instead of "take over" control. Paul tells us, *"For we are God's masterpiece. He has created us anew in Christ Jesus, so we can do the good things he planned for us long ago."* (Eph 2:10 NLT). The Master creates and commissions His masterpiece.

God Wants My Patience More Than My Plans. God's timetable considers eternity past and eternity promised folding them into His everyday plan. The psalmist, David tells us, *"Wait patiently for the Lord. Be brave and courageous. Yes, wait patiently for the Lord."* (Ps 27:14 NLT). Waiting on God enhances the work of God.

God Wants My Intercession More Than My Intervention. F.B. Meyer writes, "The greatest tragedy of life is not unanswered prayer, but unoffered prayer."[190] Eugene Peterson, in The Message, gives some insight into the apostle Paul's teaching, *"The first thing I want you to do is pray. Pray every way you know how,* *for everyone you know. Pray especially for rulers and their governments to rule well so we can be quietly about our business of living simply, in humble contemplation. This is the way our Savior God wants us to live."* (1 Tim 2:1-3 MSG) Prayer is the priority which releases God's power. Woodrow Kroll reminds us, "Fervent prayers produce phenomenal results."[191]

If there is a foolishness of God, it is still be more intelligent that my greatest insight.

God sees more than I can see.

God understands more than I understand.

God cares more than I care.

So, what God wants . . . I want.

KINGDOM THOUGHT 96: THE BIG WIN

No, despite all these things, overwhelming victory is ours through Christ, who loved us.
Romans 8:37 NLT

Lopsided Victories. Some use the term, "blowout". It's when one opponent so overwhelms the other that victory is not only anticipated, but amazing.

One of sports truly overwhelming teams was the 1901 Michigan Wolverines Football team. Impressive enough is a winning record of 11-0. But, also wins of 128-0 (Michigan v Buffalo, Oct 26), 89-0 (Michigan v Beloit, Nov 23), a Rose Bowl win of 49-0 (Michigan v Stanford, Jan 1, 1902) and no victory with less than 21 points. Even more astonishing is that the team didn't let an opponent score a single point the entire season . . . they out-scored other teams 550 to 0.[192]

Paul reminds the Christ followers in Rome that they were more than conquerors through the One who loved them. We also have the promise of overwhelming power and victory. It's not dependent on our strength or skills, but on His sacrificial love.

Overwhelming Victory Over Sin. Jesus sheds His precious blood to pay the penalty for yesterday's, today's and tomorrow's sin. His resurrection from death gives us the power to live in victory. Paul writes, "When He died, He died once to break the power of sin. But now that He lives, He lives for the glory of God." (Rom 6:10 NLT). Sin's chains no longer confine us . . . He is our chain-breaker. The apostle continues, *"Sin is no longer your master, for you no longer live under the requirements of the law. Instead, you live under the freedom of God's grace."* (Rom 6:14 NLT). Our victory is overwhelming, and His grace is great.

Overwhelming Victory Over Shame. Paul writes, *"So now there is no condemnation for those who belong to Christ Jesus."* (Rom 8:1 NLT) The enemy and his minions will shadow us with condemnation and shame us for our conduct. Shame does not survive when compassion replaces condemnation. Shaming is man's demolition of what God has built. Humiliation tears down with guilt, but honor builds up with grace. Kay Magnate encourages us, "There is no shame in being a broken man, you just have to pick up the pieces and start rebuilding."[193]

Overwhelming Victory In Suffering. Suffering is part of life. Suffering is not terminal, but temporary. In our grief, God gives us grace. Peter reminds us, *"And after you have suffered a little while, the God of all grace, who has called you to his eternal glory in Christ, will Himself restore, confirm, strengthen, and* *establish you."* (1 Pet 5:10 ESV). As Paul writes about his own life, he faces debilitating suffering. His surrender to God's sufficiency is his victorious solution, *"For the sake of Christ, then, I am content with weaknesses, insults, hardships, persecutions, and calamities. For when I am weak, then I am strong."* (2 Cor 12:10 ESV)

Overwhelming Victory Is Secure. Our destiny is one we can depend upon. Paul emphatically states, "And I am convinced that nothing can ever separate us from God's love. Neither death nor life, neither angels nor demons, neither our fears for today nor our worries about tomorrow—not even the powers of hell can separate us from God's love. No power in the sky above or in the earth below—indeed, nothing in all creation will ever be able to separate us from the love of God that is revealed in Christ Jesus our Lord." (Rom 8:38-39 NLT). There is not a think-so assumption, but a know-so affirmation. Our victory is secure.

The following lyrics are from Charles Naylor, in the early 1900's,

> *"On the winning side, I'm on the winning side,*
> *I'm on the winning side with Jesus;*
> *Though hot may be the fray,*
> *My soul can boldly say,*
> *I'm on the winning side with Jesus."*[194]

We are no longer defeated . . . we are delivered. Through opposition and obstacle, we have victory in Jesus.

Jesus makes us more than conquerors . . . we are overwhelming conquerors. We're on the winning side.

KINGDOM MOMENT 97: LIGHT

O LORD, you are my lamp. The LORD lights up my darkness.
2 Samuel 22:29 NLT

The dimmest light can illuminate the blackest darkness. Walk into a dark room, light a candle and there is an instant awareness that is realized.

The prophet Samuel writes that *"The LORD lights up [our] darkness".* When God reveals His presence, He radiates a path through our problems. In our gloom, He gives light.

Light Drives Out Darkness. The apostle John writes, *"This is the message we heard from Jesus and now declare to you: God is light, and there is no darkness in him at all."* (1 John 1:5 NLT).

Charles Gabriel penned the emphatic cry in the hymn, "Send The Light" in 1890 based on Psalm 43:3,

> "Send the Light! The blessed gospel Light; Let it shine from shore to shore! Send the Light! The blessed gospel Light: Let it shine for evermore."

Benjamin Franklin is quoted, "Instead of cursing the darkness, light a candle."[195] God's truth leads us out of darkness into the glorious light.

Light Gives Us Direction. David writes, *"Send out Your light and Your truth; let them lead me."* (Ps 43:3) In another psalm, God's word is described as a *"a lamp to my feet and a light to my path."* (Ps 119:105) The illuminating truth of God's word instructs in our moment by moment steps, as well as our monumental journeys. Jesus says, *"I am the light of the world. If you follow Me, you won't have to walk in darkness, because you will have the light that leads to life."* (John 8:12 NLT). His light always leads to life.

Light Reveals Our Destiny. Our commitment to the Light connects us with those walk in the Light. We share with other suffering saints. We connect with the faithful who face fear. We know from whence we have come and where we are going. We share a bond with those who are cleansed by Jesus's sacrifice and redemption. John reminds us, *"But if we are living in the light, as God is in the light, then we have fellowship with each other, and the blood of Jesus, his Son, cleanses us from all sin."* (1 John 1:7 NLT). Live in the light and know that you belong to Jesus and His family.

Tim Hughes wrote these lyrics in 2001. He reminds us of God's incarnate demonstration of compassion, and he rejoices in our only declaration and confession . . . "So here I am to worship . . . here I am to bow down."

"Light of the world you step down into darkness,
Opened my eyes let me see.
Beauty that makes this heart adore You,
Hope of a life spent with You."
"So here I am to worship,
Here I am to bow down,
Here I am to say that your my God.
Your altogether lovely, Altogether worthy,
Altogether wonderful to me."

The beloved disciple John sums it up, *"And the Word was made flesh, and dwelt among us, and we beheld His glory . . . His Light . . . the glory as of the only begotten of the Father, full of grace and truth."* (John 1:14)

Live in His light. Give His light. Love His light. Allow His light to redefine you.

Kingdom Thought 98: With Different Eyes

When He saw the crowds, He had compassion on them because they were confused and helpless, like sheep without a shepherd. He said to his disciples, "The harvest is great, but the workers are few."
Matthew 9:36-37 NLT

Perspective.

Writers craft it by creating word pictures.

Artist capture it in visual imagery.

Storytellers develop a community of intrigue, involvement and inspiration.

Each of these influencers move us from seeing with our own eyes to seeing with new eyes.

They change our perspective.

God also has a different way of seeing things. He looks beyond our appearance and sees our attitude. He looks deep within our heart to see our compassion and our commitment.

As God searches for a new king in Israel, He tells Samuel *"For the Lord sees not as man sees: man looks on the outward appearance, but the Lord looks on the heart."* (1 Sam 16:7 ESV)

When we see what God sees, we impact and influence our surroundings.

Eyes Of Compassion. Jesus' eyes are empathetic. Matthew writes, *"Jesus saw the huge crowd as He stepped from the boat, and He had compassion on them and healed their sick."* (Matt 14:14 NLT). When He sees their condition, He is moved with compassion. Jesus gives us an example to embrace. Luke records the longing look of a faithful father watching for a surrendered son. He writes, *"So he returned home to his father. And while he was still a long way off, his father saw him coming. Filled with love and compassion, he ran to his son, embraced him, and kissed him."* (Luke 15:20 NLT). What we see and how we respond is an indicator of our heart. John reminds us, *"If someone has enough money to live well and sees a brother or sister in need but shows no compassion—how can God's love be in that person?"* (1 John 3:17 NLT).

Eyes Of Consideration. I love Jesus' comment to His disciples . . . simple, yet profound . . . great need, but too few to meet the need. He causes them to consider, to evaluate, to process . . . *"The harvest is great, the laborers are few."* Seed planted. Soil watered. Growth beginning. The harvest is great (present tense) . . . but we don't have enough laborers. The psalmist, David reminds us, *"How blessed is he who considers the helpless; The LORD will deliver him in a day* *of trouble."* (Ps 41:1 NASB) When Jesus sees the need, He provides a solution.

Eyes Of Commitment. God's compassion compliments His commitment. The psalmist reminds us, *"O Lord, you have searched me and known me! You know when I sit down and when I rise up; you discern my thoughts from afar. You search out my path and my lying down and are acquainted with all my ways."* (Ps 139:1-3 ESV). He sees us . . . He sees all of us. God no longer sees us in our sin . . . He sees us through our Savior, His Son. T. D. Jakes writes the following words, "Beautiful! That's how mercy saw me. Though I was broken and so lost, mercy looked past all my faults. The justice of God saw what I had done. But mercy saw me through the Son. Not what I was but what I could be. That's how mercy saw me."[196] What compassion! What commitment! He looks beyond our fault and sees our need.

Our God is "El Roi" . . . the God Who sees (Gen 16:13). He sees us in our lowest valleys and on our highest mountain tops. He looks at us with eyes of compassion and commitment. We are His own.

Mike Otto writes the following lyrics:

> *"Let me see this world, dear Lord,*
> *As though I were looking through Your eyes.*
> *A world of men who don't want You Lord,*
> *But a world for which You died."*
> *"Let me kneel with You in the garden,*
> *Blur my eyes with tears of agony;*
> *For if once I could see this world the way You see,*
> *I just know I'd serve You more faithfully."*[197]

Compassion moves.

Consideration measures.

Commitment mandates.

See today as God sees it. See it with your heart and with hope. His perspective is our priority.

KINGDOM THOUGHT 99: SURVIVING

So be truly glad. There is wonderful joy ahead, even though you must endure many trials for a little while.
1 Peter 1:6 NLT

There's a word in this verse that is challenging . . . the word "must".

Peter tells us that we "must endure many trials for a little while". But, why?

Elizabeth Elliott writes, "I am not a theologian or a scholar, but I am very aware of the fact that pain is necessary to all of us. In my own life, I think I can honestly say that out of the deepest pain has come the strongest conviction of the presence of God and the love of God."[198]

We find grace in our grieving.

We find mercy in our mess.

We find His presence in our pain.

The Response. Peter tells us to be "truly glad." A heart felt response of praise gives us a hopeful reality in our pain. James reminds us, *"Count it all joy, my brothers, when you meet trials of various kinds, for you know that the testing of your faith produces steadfastness."* (Jam 1:2-3 ESV). Being steadfast means, we are secure even in our struggles. In our chaos and conflict, we have confidence that God is in control.

The Reason. Peter reminds us that there is a purpose for our pain. The apostle writes, *"These trials will show that your faith is genuine. It is being tested as fire tests and purifies gold—though your faith is far more precious than mere gold. So, when your faith remains strong through many trials, it will bring you much praise and glory and honor on the day when Jesus Christ is revealed to the whole world."* (1 Peter 1:7 NLT). Our trust is in God's compassion and care. We are tested and God is true in our trials. And, there is hope that rises from our hurt. Paul reminds us, *"For I consider that the sufferings of this present time are not worth comparing with the glory that is to be revealed to us"*. (Rom 8:18 ESV)

The Resolve. We know that *"there is wonderful joy ahead."* (1 Pet 1:6). There is a beauty that is born from our burdens. Elizabeth Kubler-Ross writes, "The most beautiful people we have known are those who have known defeat, known suffering, known struggle, known loss, and have found their way out of the depths. These persons have an appreciation, a sensitivity, and an understanding of life that fills them with compassion, gentleness, and a deep loving concern. Beautiful people do not just happen."[199]

Our pain may be prevalent, but it is not permanent. C. S. Lewis encourages us, "God, who foresaw your tribulation, has specially armed you to go through it, not without pain but without stain."[200]

Pain and injury often leave scars reminding us that we suffered, but also that we survived. Tom Paterson says, "You never get over it, but you will get through it."[201]

Struggling? Suffering? Shaken?

Strive to survive and "be truly glad because there is a wonderful day ahead."

Kingdom Thought 100: Doors

To the angel of the church in Philadelphia write the following: "This is the solemn pronouncement of the Holy One, the True One, who holds the key of David, who opens doors no one can shut, and shuts doors no one can open."
Revelation 3:7 NET

We've all been there . . . not having the faith to move forward or being hindered by the fear of what may lay ahead.

Fear paralyzes. It can stop us "dead" in our tracks.

I often wonder if God is leading . . . if He is preparing a way for me . . . if God is really opening a door.

God's guidance is governed by His grace. He will never lead us where He will not love us. God never shuts a door that He desires to be open and He never opens a door that He deems unsafe. His working is guided by His will and wisdom.

God's Will. The historical and prophetic message for the church of Philadelphia looked back and looked forward. John quotes Jesus, *"I know your deeds. See, I have placed before you an open door that no one can shut. I know that you have little strength, yet you have kept My word and have not denied My name."* (Rev 3:8 NIV) We often depend on our smarts, our own skill and our own strength to move the proverbial door. Yet God promises us that even in our weakest times, He opens doors in our lives that no one can shut. Following God's will may seem foolish to some. But Peter reminds us, *"It is God's will that your honorable lives should silence those ignorant people who make foolish accusations against you."* (1 Pet 2:15 NLT)

God's Wisdom. In our humanness, we are limited in understanding the holiness of God. The Father sent His Son to defeat our sin and show us Truth and Wisdom. Paul writes, *"God has united you with Christ Jesus. For our benefit God made Him to be wisdom itself. Christ made us right with God; He made us pure and holy, and He freed us from sin."* (1 Cor 1:30 NLT). If we are empty of wisdom, God will fill us up. James reminds us, *"If you need wisdom, ask our generous God, and he will give it to you. He will not rebuke you for asking."* (Jam 1:5 NLT)

Our Wanting. Our desire determines our destiny. The psalmist writes, "Trust in the LORD and do good. Then you will live safely in the land and prosper. Take delight in the LORD, and He will give you your heart's desires. Commit everything you do to the LORD. Trust Him, and He will help you." (Ps 37:3-5 NLT) It becomes easier to walk through God's open doors when our wants are aligned with His will. This only occurs when we think like He thinks and trust in His wise leadership. Our thoughts are transformed, and our will is reworked. Paul encourages us, *"Don't copy the behavior and customs of this world, but let God transform you into a new person by changing the way you think. Then you will learn to know God's will for you, which is good and pleasing and perfect."* (Rom 12:2 NLT)

In 2002, Keith Getty and Stuart Townend wrote the following lyrics to a new hymn, "In Christ Alone":

> *"No guilt in life, no fear in death, this is the power of Christ in me;*
> *From life's first cry to final breath, Jesus commands my destiny.*
> *No power of hell, no scheme of man, can ever pluck me from His hand:*
> *Till He returns or calls me home, here in the power of Christ I'll stand."*

Allow Jesus to open and shut the doors in your life.

He will never deny you, despise you, distract you or disappoint you.

You can stand in Him . . . ALONE.

Kingdom Thought 101: It's Paid In Full

God made Him who had no sin to be sin for us, so that in Him we might become the righteousness of God.
2 Corinthians 5:21 NIV

In the greatest commutation story ever, the completely innocent takes the place of the condemned immoral. God takes our wrong and places it on His Son. In doing so, we become right in our standing with God. Sometimes that explanation sounds a bit too spiritual to make a daily impact on the way we live and think.

This can be a challenging concept to grasp. The reasoning of God and the result we experience is beyond comprehension.

So, try this one . . . God takes all of our debt . . . everything we owe . . . all that we beg, borrow and steal in order to be approved and accepted. Even with all of our efforts, we hopelessly come up short. God transfers all of our liabilities to Jesus. The debt is so great that Jesus can only pay for it with His life. He willingly pays for it . . . and makes us debt free. When our debt is paid, God makes it possible for us to be a part of His family. He doesn't stop there . . .

He Gives Us The Inheritance Of His Son. We are part of God's family . . . through tragic times and triumphant times. Paul writes, *"For His Spirit joins with our spirit to affirm that we are God's children. And since we are His children, we are His heirs. In fact, together with Christ we are heirs of God's glory. But if we are to share His glory, we must also share His suffering."* (Rom 8:16-17 NLT)

He Provides Us With A Home That Will Never Be Taken Away. In these challenging economic times, many have lost their residence. These are places in which we create memories, moments and meaning. Our everyday house pales in comparison to our eternal home. Jesus tells us, *"In My Father's house are many rooms. If it were not so, would I have told you that I go to prepare a place for you? And if I go and prepare a place for you, I will come again and will take you to Myself, that where I am you may be also."* (Jn 14:2-3 ESV)

He Promises To Take Care Of Our Needs. In times of sparing, Jesus supplies. Paul encourages us, *"And my God will supply every need of yours according to his riches in glory in Christ Jesus."* (Phil 4:19 ESV)

He Clothes Us With Righteousness. They say that clothes make the man (or woman). The prophet Isaiah writes, *"I am overwhelmed with joy in the LORD my God! For he has dressed me with the clothing of salvation and draped me in a robe of righteousness . . ."* (Is 61:10 NLT)

He pays our debt and we will never owe Him a penny. Paul reminds us, *"He canceled the record of the charges against us and took it away by nailing it to the cross."* (Col 2:14 NLT)

So, the next time you use that credit card, write that student loan payment, make that car payment, send in the mortgage payment, or get a copy of your credit score . . . don't be discouraged or disappointed . . . decide to thank God for the eternal debt that Jesus paid.

It feels good to be eternally debt free in Jesus.

SOURCES

[1] Greg Nemer, http://reallifepurpose.org/what-are-defining-moments/ June 15, 2012

[2] Jonathan Aitken, John Newton: From Grace to Amazing Grace, Continuum, 2007

[3] A.W. Tozer, The Pursuit Of God, 1948

[4] Jerry Bridges, Who Am I? Identity in Christ (Adelphi, Maryland: Cruciform Press, 2012, 92-93

[5] Alexander Whyte, "The Apostle Paul", 1903

[6] Rick Warren, The Purpose Driven Life, Zondervan, 2002

[7] "Saint Augustine." BrainyQuote.com. http://www.brainyquote.com/quotes/s/saintaugus105351.html

[8] Sarah Young, Jesus Calling. Thomas Nelson, 2004

[9] Ibid

[10] https://www.huffpost.com/entry/why-do-we-blink-so-much-mental-rest_n_2377720, December 30, 2012

[11] https://dictionary.cambridge.org/us/

[12] https://insight.org/resources/daily-devotional/individual/the-authenticity-of-our-words, July 14, 2018

[13] https://au.reachout.com/mental-fitness/self-talk-and-self-awareness

[14] Erich Fromm (2014). "The Erich Fromm Reader: Readings Selected and Edited by Rainer Funk", p.105, Open Road Media

[15] Matthew Henry Commentary, Zondervan Academic, 1961

[16] Richard Whately (1839). "Essays on Some of the Dangers to Christian Faith"

[17] Pope John Paul II, The Biography, April 2, 2014

[18] T.W. Manson, The Church's Ministry, March 1949

[19] Teaching from Jonathan Falwell, Senior Pastor, Thomas Road Baptist Church

[20] Michael Bernard Beckwith, The Answer Is You, 2009

[21] Rob Kuban, Christ-Centered Contentment, 2010

[22] Laozi, Chinese Philosopher, 249 BC

[23] Pearl S. Buck, 1892-1973

[24] Henry Donald Maurice Spence-Jones, Joseph S. Exell, The Pulpit Commentary, 1950

[25] Abraham Lincoln, 16th President of the United States, 1809-1865

[26] James McFall, Thank God I Am Free, 1969

[27] Sir Winston Churchill, 1874-1965

[28] Brent Byerman, Spiritual Warfare, Lake Magdalene United Methodist Church

[29] The wisdom of Frank (Rusty) D. Goodwin

[30] Judson W. Van de Venter (1855-1939), I Surrender All

[31] Martin Luther King, Jr., The Three Dimensions of the Complete Life, Covenant Baptist Church, Chicago, IL, 1967

[32] J. Vernon McGee, Through The Bible Radio, 1904-1998

[33] Alexander Whyte, "The Apostle Paul", 1903

[34] Francis Shaeffer, How Shall We Then Live, 1976

[35] Westminster Shorter Catechism, Westminster Assembly, 1649

[36] Oscar Wilde, The Soul Of A Man Under Socialism, 1891

[37] Albert E. Brumley, The World Is Not My Home, 1937

[38] Herbert Lockyer, All The Promises In The Bible, 1962

[39] Chris Rademaker, Jodi King, Seth Mosley, He Is With Us, Warner Chappell Music, Inc,

Capitol Christian Music Group, 2013
[40] Fannie Flagg, I Still About You: A Novel, Ballentine Books, 2011
[41] Norman Vincent Peale, Positive Thinking Everyday: An Inspiration For Each Day Of The Year, Touchstone Publishing, 1993
[42] Sarah Young, Jesus Calling. Thomas Nelson, 2004
[43] Mark A. Hall, Stephen Curtis Chapman, The Voice Of Truth, 2003
[44] Samuel Chadwick, The Path Of Prayer, 1931
[45] John Bunyun, The Works Of That Eminent Servant Of Christ, Volume One, 1692
[46] Attributed to Diane Sawyer, ABC Anchor, (1945-)
[47] The Wisdom Of Matthew Wilmington, LCN Regional Meeting, Lynchburg, VA, 2018
[48] Liz Bohannon, Work As Worship Simulcast, February 22, 2019
[49] Tim Keller, Counterfeit Gods: When The Empty Promises Of Love, Money and Power Let You Down, 2010
[50] George MacDonald, The Musicians Quest, Chapter XVI, Change of Scene, 1824-1905
[51] Patrick Lai, Really, Work Is Worship, http://businessasmission.com/really-work-is-worship, July 4 2016
[52] https://www.nobelpeaceprize.org/
[53] Eleanor Roosevelt, Voice of America broadcast, November 11 1951
[54] Mother Teresa (Mary Teresa Bojaxhiu), Order Of The Smile, www.catholic.org, 1910-1997
[55] Lance Witt, Replenish, Baker Books, 2011
[56] Charles Swindoll, The Deepest Need, Insight For Living, March 22 2018
[57] C.S. Lewis, A Grief Observed, 1961
[58] O.A. Lambert, Sacred Songs, 1958
[59] Corallie Buchanan, Watch Out! Godly Women on the Loose, 2009
[60] Charles Swindoll, The Grace Awakening, 1990
[61] Matt Redman, Never Once, 10,000 Reasons, 2011
[62] The Wisdom of Richard Scales
[63] David Bly, We All Do Better: Economic Priorities For A Land Of Opportunity, 2016
[64] Og Mandino, The Og Group, 1923 - 1996
[65] Ralph Waldo Emerson, American Essayist and Author, 1803-1882
[66] Adoniram Judson, American Congregationalist and Missionary, 1788-1850
[67] Tony Evans, Kingdom Man: Every Man's Destiny, Every Woman's Dream, 2012
[68] Jana Magruder, Nothing Less, Lifeway, 2017
[69] Mother Teresa (Mary Teresa Bojaxhiu), Order Of The Smile, www.catholic.org, 1910-1997
[70] J.I. Packer, Knowing God, 1973
[71] George Mueller, Answers To Prayer, 1895
[72] A.W. Tozer, The Pursuit Of God, 1948
[73] Ibid
[74] Bill and Gloria Gaither, Joy Comes In The Morning, 2001
[75] Alexander Graham Bell, 1847 - 1922
[76] David Garcia, Ben Glover, Christopher Stevens, Overcomer, 2013
[77] Charles H. Spurgeon, Letters To My Students, 1866
[78] S.D. Gordon, Quiet Talks On Prayer, 1904
[79] Charles H. Spurgeon, 1834 - 1892
[80] Jim Hill, What A Day That Will Be, 1953

[81] Sir Thomas More, 1748-1535
[82] Philip Melanchthen, 1497-1560, https://spartacus-educational.com
[83] John Wooden, 1910-2010, https://www.thewoodeneffect.com/motivational-quotes-john-wooden
[84] Augustine of Hippo (Aurelius Augustinus Hipponensis), 354-430, Augustine's Retractions, Book 2
[85] Charles Haddon Spurgeon, Treasury Of David, 1869
[86] John Bunyun, The Works Of That Eminent Servant Of Christ, Volume One, 1692
[87] Shirley Ann Caesar-Williams & Albertina Walker, Peace In The Midst Of The Storm, 1988
[88] Pope Francis, https://twitter.com/pontifex/status/351989207083917312, 2013
[89] Ibid
[90] D.L. Moody as told by Mr. Fitt, The Presbyterian Banner, Vol 93, Page 9, August 9 1906
[91] Attributed to both Joseph P. Kennedy (1888-1969) and Knute Rockne (1888-1931)
[92] Franklin D. Roosevelt (1882-1945), 32nd United States President
[93] Attributed to Winston Churchill (1874-1965)
[94] James E. Paino, He's Able, 1958
[95] Scotty Smith, Everyday Prayers, Baker Books, 2011
[96] Ibid
[97] Ibid
[98] Stephen M. R. Covey, The Speed Of Trust, Simon Schuster, 2006
[99] https://www.opednews.com/articles/Little-girl-and-her-father-by-YJ-Draiman-110109-269.html
[100] Oswald Chambers, My Utmost For His Highest, 1927
[101] Ibid
[102] Diana Pavlac Glyer, Clay In The Potter's Hands, 2011
[103] Henry Spencer-Jones, The Complete Pulpit Commentary, Vol 8, Delmarva Publications, 2013
[104] Max Lucado, In The Eye Of The Storm, Thomas Nelson Publishing, 2012
[105] Scott Wesley Brown, He Will Carry You, 1995
[106] Reggie White, In The Trenches, Thomas Nelson, 1997
[107] Ibid
[108] Attributed to Abraham Lincoln (1809-1865), 16th President of the United States
[109] John Piper, How Did Jesus Learn Obedience (Hebrews 5:7-9), Desiring God, 2018
[110] Rhea F. Miller, I'd Rather Have Jesus, 1922
[111] Ibid
[112] C.S. Lewis, Voyage To Venus, Macmillen Press, 1968
[113] Notes from Business As Mission Conference, Feb 2019
[114] Arthur Walkington Pink, 1886-1952
[115] Ibid
[116] October 2, 2016, https://billygraham.org/devotion/a-daily-process/
[117] Henry Ford, 1863-1947, https://www.quotes.net/quote/42253
[118] Ibid
[119] Gary Paxton, You Can Build A Bridge, 1975
[120] Rick Warren, The Purpose Driven Life, 2010
[121] Ibid
[122] Emma Louise Parry, Woman In The Reformation, Lutheran Publication, 1882, page 38
[123] Charles Bridges, An Exposition On The Book Of Provers, 1847, page 531

[124] Thane Rosenbaum, Payback: The Case For Revenge, 2013, page 84
[125] William O. Stevens, Stoic Ethics: Epictetus And Happiness In Freedom, 2007
[126] Martin Luther King, Jr., Acceptance Speech for Nobel Peace Prize, December 10, 1964
[127] Ernest Hemingway, Finca Vigia, 1947, Hemingway Preservation Foundation
[128] Dr. A. D. Williams, (1933-1990) NFL Player
[129] Ralph Waldo Emerson (1803-1882) an American essayist, lecturer, and poet
[130] Mark Twain Quotes. (n.d.). BrainyQuote.com. Retrieved August 13, 2019, from BrainyQuote.com Web site: https://www.brainyquote.com/quotes/mark_twain_120156
[131] Frank Tyger (1929-2011) https://franktyger.info/
[132] Leonard Ravenhill, Why Revival Tarries, 1959, page 74
[133] Ibid
[134] David F. Wells, Losing Our Virtue: Why The Church Must Recover Its Moral Virtue, 1998, page 204
[135] Ibid
[136] Tommy Walker, When I Don't Know What To Do, Break Through, 2006
[137] John F. Kennedy, 1917-1963, Presidential Inaugural Address, 1961
[138] Joseph Campbell, The Power Of Myth, 1988, page 123
[139] John Bryce, The Bulletin, 1912, page 39
[140] Ibid
[141] Rick Joyner, The Final Quest, 2010
[142] Cheryl A. Bachelder, Dare To Serve: How To Drive Superior Results By Serving Others, Berrett-Koehler Publishers, 2015
[143] Ibid
[144] Pearl Strachan Hurd, Selected Poems By Pearl Strachan Hurd, 1946
[145] Ibid
[146] Jodi Picoult, The Story Teller, 2016
[147] Ann Voskamp, One Thousand Gifts: A Dare to Live Fully Right Where You Are, Zondervan, 2011
[148] John Gill, John Gill's Exposition Of The Entire Bible, Proverbs, 1746-1763
[149] Elizabeth Elliot, A Path Through Suffering, Baker Books, 1990
[150] George Washington, 1732-1799, First President Of The United States
[151] Ibid
[152] Ibid
[153] Kenneth Wuest, The New Testament: An Expanded Translation, 1961
[154] Ibid
[155] Ibid
[156] Max Lucado, Experiencing the Heart of Jesus: Knowing His Heart, Feeling His Love, 2003
[157] Timothy Keller, The Prodigal God: Recovering the Heart of the Christian Faith, 2003
[158] Shauna Niequist, Present Over Perfect, Zondervan, 2016
[159] Steve Maraboli, Unapologetically You: Reflections on Life and the Human Experience, A Better Today, 2013
[160] Israelmore Ayivor, https://www.goodreads.com/quotes/841243-the-only-way-to-make-a-spoilt-machine-work-again
[161] Pamela Rose Williams, https://www.whatchristianswanttoknow.com/love-one-a
[162] Barbara De Angelis, Real Moments, Delacorte Press, 1995, page 160

[163] *Attribute to Jimmy Larche, www.jimmylarche.com*
[164] *Ibid*
[165] *Attributed to Pope John XXIII (Angelo Giuseppe Roncalli) November 25 1881 – June 3 1963 https://www.quotetab.com/quotes/by-pope-john-xxiii/*
[166] *Robert Jamieson, A.R. Fausset and David Brown, A Commentary Critical And Explanatory of the Old and New Testament, 1872*
[167] *John Ciardi Quotes. (n.d.). BrainyQuote.com. Retrieved August 15, 2019, from BrainyQuote.com Web site: https://www.brainyquote.com/quotes/john_ciardi_406998*
[168] *Dietrich Bonhoeffer, Letters and Papers from Prison, 1951*
[169] *Helen Keller Quotes. (n.d.). BrainyQuote.com. Retrieved August 15, 2019, from BrainyQuote.com Web site: https://www.brainyquote.com/quotes/helen_keller_384608*
[170] *Ibid*
[171] *Felice Leonardo Buscaglia, Love, 1972*
[172] *https://goop.com/wellness/spirituality/what-dreams-mean/*
[173] *Author unknown. But, it's on Pinterest quite a few times.*
[174] *Mitch Albom, Tuesdays With Morrie: An Old Man, A Young Man, and Life's Greatest Lessons, 1997*
[175] *Ibid*
[176] *A Profile of Theodore Roosevelt, The American Monthly Review of Reviews, 1900*
[177] *J. Hampton Keathley III, Studies In The Life Of Elijah, 1995*
[178] *Erwin W. Lutzer, Failure: The Back Door To Success, Moody, 1988*
[179] *Ibid*
[180] *J. Oswald Sanders, Spiritual Leadership, 1966*
[181] *https://www.azquotes.com/picture-quotes/Thomas A. Edison*
[182] *Attributed to A.A. Conrad, https://thoughts-about-god.com/quotes_/quotes-god*
[183] *Henri Nouwen, The Return Of The Prodigal Son, 1992*
[184] *https://www.skipmoen.com/2009/04/the-crucial-difference/*
[185] *https://www.huffpost.com/entry/finding-harmony-in-2015-p_b_6755202*
[186] *Ibid*
[187] *https://issuu.com/blessedmagazine/docs/blessed_magazine_february__march_20*
[188] *https://livingontheedge.org/2000/01/02/does-god-really-care-about-me*
[189] *Alistair Begg, https://www.truthforlife.org/resources/sermon/you-can-not-be-serious/*
[190] *https://www.azquotes.com/author/19129-F_B_Meyer/tag/prayer*
[191] *https://prayforrevival.wordpress.com/2017/06/17/woodrow-kroll-on-fervent-prayer/*
[192] *https://en.wikipedia.org/wiki/1901_Michigan_Wolverines_football_team*
[193] *https://kingsolomonsmine.blogspot.com/2017/05/theres-no-shame-in-been-broken-man_20.html*
[194] *Charles W. Naylor, I'm On The Winning Side, 1921*
[195] *https://quotefancy.com/quote/10649/Benjamin-Franklin-Instead-of-cursing-the-darkness-light-a-candle*
[196] *Lyrics by Geron La Ray Davis and Rebecca C. Davis, Mercy Saw Me, 1997*
[197] *Looking Through His Eyes, Words and music by Mike Otto arranged by David T. CLydesdale; copyright 1979 by John T. Benson Publishing Company*
[198] *http://womenofchristianity.com/quotes/elisabeth-elliot-quotes/*
[199] *Elisabeth Kübler-Ross, On Death and Dying, 1969*
[200] *Ibid*
[201] *Tom Paterson, Living The Life You Were Meant To Live, 1989*

Made in the USA
Columbia, SC
30 January 2022